PRAISE FOR
ELEMENTAL LOVE STYLES

"Through the self-awareness that Dr. Craig's book gave us, my boyfriend and I were able to relish our differences, celebrate our similarities, and negotiate the tough waters in between. He taught us that honesty about our deepest needs is the best policy and the only way to a satisfying, truly intimate relationship. It saved us!"

—Donna Powers, screenwriter of *The Italian Job*

"Dr. Craig Martin is profoundly insightful—he knows what he is talking about. He is truly a healer's healer. His book [*Elemental Love Styles*] is a true standout among a sea of relationship manuals. Finally, someone speaking for the highest vision of love and relationships rather than the lowest common denominator. This guide is filled with insights that, like a laser beam, light up the deepest recesses of your soul and your relationship; allow it to transform yours."

—Stacey Wolf, astrologer and author of *Never Throw Rice at a Pisces*

"Dr. Craig is a wise and insightful voice for relationships."

—Michelle Orrego, KTLA, Los Angeles television producer

"*Elemental Love Styles* opens your eyes to all aspects of creating and maintaining a deep relationship within yourself and ultimately with all others. Dr. Craig encourages you to learn your element style and provides you a guide to self-discovery and personal growth. *Elemental Love Styles* is perfect for anyone eager to develop a love within and be able to illuminate that love in all areas of life."

—**Robin Marvel,** author of *Awakening Consciousness: A Girl's Guide!* and *Awakening Consciousness: A Boy's Guide!*

"Dr. Craig is a gifted human being who has a unique ability to understand both what you need—physically, spiritually, and emotionally—and what you need to let go of so you can thrive in your life. *Elemental Love Styles* is similarly smart and intuitive, a guide to self-discovery that not only sets you on a path to understanding your own needs for love but also to finding the love inside yourself."

—**Alanna Fincke,** former editor in chief of *Body+Soul* magazine

ELEMENTAL LOVE STYLES

ELEMENTAL LOVE STYLES

FIND COMPATIBILITY AND CREATE A LASTING RELATIONSHIP

DR. CRAIG MARTIN

ATRIA PAPERBACK
New York London Toronto Sydney

BEYOND WORDS
Hillsboro, Oregon

ATRIA PAPERBACK
A Division of Simon & Schuster, Inc.
1230 Avenue of the Americas
New York, NY 10020

BEYOND WORDS
20827 N.W. Cornell Road, Suite 500
Hillsboro, Oregon 97124-9808
503-531-8700 / 503-531-8773 fax
www.beyondword.com

Managing editor: Lindsay S. Brown
Copyeditor: Henry Covey
Proofreader: Jade Chan
Design: Devon Smith
Composition: William H. Brunson Typography Services

First Atria Paperback/Beyond Words trade paperback edition February 2010

ATRIA PAPERBACK and colophon are trademarks of Simon & Schuster, Inc.
Beyond Words Publishing is a division of Simon & Schuster, Inc.

For more information about special discounts for bulk purchases,
please contact Simon & Schuster Special Sales at 1-866-506-1949 or
business@simonandschuster.com.

The Simon & Schuster Speakers Bureau can bring authors to your live event.
For more information or to book an event, contact the Simon & Schuster Speakers Bureau at 1-866-248-3049 or visit our website at www.simonspeakers.com.

Manufactured in the United States of America

10 9 8 7 6 5 4 3 2 1

Library of Congress Cataloging-in-Publication Data:

Martin, Craig,
     Elemental love styles : find compatibility and create a lasting relationship /
Craig Martin.
          p.   cm.
     1. Intimacy (Psychology).   2. Love.   I. Title.

     BF575.I5M283   2010
     158.2—dc22

                                                                    2009036686

ISBN 978-1-58270-256-8
ISBN 978-1-4391-7137-0 (ebook)

The corporate mission of Beyond Words Publishing, Inc.: *Inspire to Integrity*

For Dan

Contents

Acknowledgments

Writing a book about lasting relationships, change, and personal growth is not done alone. It begins by recognizing that everyone who has touched my life has contributed in some way to the text. The book's concept and all its contents were developed in the presence of those people who have shaped me. For all of them, I am truly grateful.

That being said, there are individuals who deserve to be mentioned specifically.

I want to thank my parents, Jim and Barbara, for their endless support and love—it carries me through both the joy and the confusion; my sister, Deborah, her husband, Greg, and their family for their understanding, generosity, and commitment; my brother Robert for his courageous choices to grow in such positive ways; and my brother David, his wife, Kate, and their family for being anchors of positivity and encouragement. Also, I can't forget Abby, our Old English, whose love has taught me so much about inner growth.

Acknowledgments

In addition, thanks go out to Ayres for getting me started, Ellynne for caring so sincerely, Alanna for her friendship, and Melanie for her insight, skill, and guidance. Thanks also to my agent, Krista Goering, for her faith and spiritual depth; my publicist, Lisa Elia, for her dedication; Cynthia Black, Richard Cohn, and Marie Hix of Beyond Words Publishing for believing in me; my Beyond Words team—Danielle Marshall, Whitney Quon, Devon Smith, Bill Brunson, Brian Danziger, and Henry Covey—and Lindsay Brown, my editor, for guiding the completion of this process. Also, thank you to Judith Curr of Simon & Schuster for her confidence in me.

To all the people who helped with the Elemental Style Quiz and the Dr. Craig letters—Lisa, Carter, Savannah, Chris and Haydie, Wendy and Craig, Cathy and Robert, Justin and Heather, Cheryl and Richie, Denise, Cheryl R., Helaine, Carol, Raine, Kaneisha, Jemaja, Susan, Pat, Bibi, Jean, Stacey, Stephanie, Laura, Christine, Len, Mandy, Georgie, Deb and Charlie, Paula, Meredith, Parker, Shaunna, Michelle, Naomi, Lyndsey, Claudette, Dennis, Art, Lauren, and Joy—I am grateful.

And then I want to thank Dan for holding my hand, for meeting my deeper needs, for listening, and for loving me so honestly.

For all this, I am blessed.

Introduction

Why haven't I found my life partner?
Why isn't my marriage working out?
How do I manage the hard parts of a good relationship?

If these questions sound familiar, you're not alone. Many people struggle to find happiness in relationships but have no idea how to make things better.

Elemental Love Styles will reveal how to identify your deeper needs in a relationship. When you know your deeper needs, you'll better understand how to find your heart's desire. If you're in a challenging relationship, the book provides intimacy skills that will help you improve communication and create more positive interactions with your partner. Best of all, you'll learn how inner growth can lead to a deeper, more fulfilling relationship.

Elemental Love Styles is your guide for self-discovery. I originally wrote it as my own guide to understanding why my relationships worked or didn't work. But after I began to share my thoughts with friends and family members, I realized that *Elemental Love Styles* could help others as well.

Before we get started on the journey to a happier relationship, I'd like to introduce myself, share some of my experiences and insights, and explain how I came to write this book.

For over twenty years, I have worked as a holistic healer and spiritual advisor. During many of those years, I was a practicing chiropractor and homeopath, as well as an interfaith minister and relationship counselor.

I opened my practice in 1988 and was well established by the mid-1990s. Everything was going great. I loved my work, felt I was making a difference in people's lives, and was doing well financially. My personal life, I thought, was good. I was in a long-term relationship with a supportive partner, and we were building a life together.

After seven years, I realized that my relationship was not what it had appeared to be. When the truth came out, we broke up. Let's just say that he wanted activities outside the relationship that didn't fit with my idea of commitment. The breakup left me feeling disillusioned and devastated. Seven years is a long time to invest in a relationship that doesn't work out.

After the breakup, I spent more time at my weekend home in the Catskill Mountains of upstate New York. I had a rustic old farmhouse set in beautiful surroundings that afforded the isolation I needed for meditation and reflection. The setting served as a perfect retreat from the hectic world of my New York City practice. I loved the natural atmosphere and welcomed the remoteness and solitude with no TV or computer. During those weekends, I did a lot of thinking, especially about my failed relationship.

One day, as I sat on the porch and looked down the road, I had a feeling of overwhelming expansiveness and godly presence. I started to think about my relationships—with my former partner as well as with my friends, family, colleagues, and clients, including people who came to me for spiritual and relationship counseling. As I sat on the porch, deep in thought, I asked myself why people so often experienced miscommunication, misunderstanding, and a lack of compatibility in relationships.

An answer shot into my mind: *People love in different ways.*

This was a revelation. People actually have different styles of loving.

I thought about specific people I knew and worked with, especially those with relationship problems. I realized how each person's love style affected his or her relationship. When the styles clashed or someone's needs weren't met, misunderstandings and arguments often ensued.

I wondered whether it was possible to categorize or group these love styles. If so, how? What were the love styles? How many were there? How could they be described?

For the next ten years, I looked for answers. For me, it was a time of introspection and self-discovery. Along the way, I had a few more short-lived relationships, mainly with people who were distant or unavailable. Why did I keep picking the same type? Why wasn't I choosing someone whose love style was compatible with mine?

In 2003 I fell head-over-heels crazy in love with someone I believed was finally "the one." He had all the trappings—good looks, a good job, and all the right extras. But in only a few months, I felt insecure, confused, and confined. I came to the painful realization that I just couldn't engage in these kinds of relationship dramas anymore.

I wondered if I was destined to never have a partner and always remain alone. To me, this was a bleak thought. I truly wanted to find my life partner. I knew that something had to change, and the change had to start with me. First of all, I needed to find some answers and gain more insight into myself.

For advice, I turned to one of my chiropractic clients, a kindhearted, caring priest I had known for several years. When I explained my lover's inability to articulate his feelings, make himself available, or make me feel valued, Father Ben responded, "Perhaps he's not meeting your deeper needs for love."

Ding, ding, ding, ding, ding! It was as if a thousand alarm clocks went off in my head and heart at the same time. That was when it all came together.

Perhaps he's not meeting your deeper needs for love.

Father Ben's words cascaded around me. I felt as if I'd spent years floating on a raft that had finally come to shore.

Yes, this was the answer. I needed to find someone who could meet my deeper needs.

Father Ben waited for me to say something, but I was too stunned to respond. I just sat there in silence as the past ten years, my failed long-term partnership, and all my relationships raced through my mind.

I thought, Even the most recent relationship, the supposed love of my life, hadn't met my deeper needs, and neither had any of the others.

I asked myself, What are my deeper needs?

I realized that I needed a partner to share life with, a person I could trust, somebody smart and nurturing, someone I felt connected with spiritually, emotionally, and physically.

My deeper needs were not necessarily to be with someone with looks or wealth, though I had explored my share of that and had ended up in superficial relationships with unavailable people. Even chemistry, the much-sought-after ingredient for relationship bliss, while important, isn't about love.

Whoa, I told myself. Wake up.

You are looking for a healthy relationship; you are looking for a commitment-oriented partner, a spiritual union. What is that really going to look like?

During my ten-year journey, I had been seeking a healthy, loving relationship, but I was like a traveler without a map. I could never reach my destination and find the right person because I had no guidelines to lead me there. All along, I just needed to look for someone who could meet my deeper needs. The answer was so simple, but it had eluded me for years and years.

It wasn't until Father Ben said, "Perhaps he's not meeting your deeper needs for love," that everything fell into place.

As I thought about my past relationships, I focused on each person's love style and understood why he wasn't a good match for me.

I also gained insight into myself. I realized that my happiness depended on finding someone who could offer what I needed, someone whose deeper needs I could meet.

After months of self-reflection, it became clear that before I could love another person and receive love in return, I had to better understand myself and my deeper needs. To gain greater self-knowledge, I decided to dig deeper into the concept of love styles and why people love in different ways.

As I searched for a way to categorize the love styles, it occurred to me that I already had the answer. Through my lifelong study of astrology and Western mysticism, I'd learned that the world could be divided into four elements—fire, air, water, and earth—each with a set of distinct characteristics. While the elements provide a way to understand the outer world, they also offer insight into the inner world of human personality.

I'm sure you've heard people called "fiery types" or "light and breezy," or someone who "goes with the flow" or someone who's "solid as a rock." When we use these expressions, we're unconsciously designating people as a certain elemental type—fire, air, water, or earth. Of course, these are the good aspects of the elemental types, but there is also the flip side—"hotheaded," "airhead," "all wet," or "stick in the mud." The point is that the elements can help explain human personality in both its positive and negative aspects.

When I realized that the elements could elucidate the different ways that people love, *Elemental Love Styles* was born. By looking at groups of people with similar traits and understanding what each set of individuals had in common, I was able to categorize people into four elemental styles. Based on these elemental love styles, people love in different ways and have deeper needs specific to their elemental types. The big payoff for all this work and study was that I began to understand my own deeper needs more clearly.

A few months later, I found, for the first time in my life, someone who met, and continues to meet, my deeper needs for love, and whose deeper needs I can meet. I discovered that the right person is the one who allows me to look at my complete self and encourages me to grow. He not only encourages my growth, but I can finally say that my partner brings out the best in me.

Love became a personal realization; when I finally found myself in it, I knew what I had been looking for all along. Rather than waiting for some vision of perfection to enter my life, I finally understood what love is about.

It amazes me that some people know this from the start. They find love early in life and commit to it right away. And when I say "find love," I don't mean that they've found "some person." I mean that they found love inside themselves. They discovered that love is the act of loving. I suspect those lucky folks already understood what they most deeply needed. They always knew what they could offer someone in a loving relationship. From there, it's easy. Then, and only then, is it possible to find the right person to love.

Through my journey, experiences, studies, introspection, and work as a relationship counselor, I've developed, explored, and tested the concepts that have resulted in the book you now hold in your hands. By finding someone who meets my deeper needs, I can be in a truly intimate relationship, one that encourages my personal inner growth and guides me toward my potential.

In some ways, I wish I had written this book sooner. I might have found my heart's desire all the sooner. But, as they say, timing is everything, and I'm so happy to share this with you now.

As a part of the learning process in the book, I have included dialogues between couples. These dialogues are simple examples of how couples work it out together and grow for the better.

I want to thank my readers for the opportunity to include in the text relationships between all people. Gender and sexual orientation are not issues in *Elemental Love Styles*. My intention to include straight, gay, and lesbian couples in these dialogues is not to shock anyone. They are here for validation and reality's sake. All people in relationships work it out together. The characters in the dialogues can be whatever religion, race, political view, or sexual orientation you want them to be. The "working it out" is the same.

Elemental Love Styles is intended for people ready to have their consciousness expanded through greater knowledge of themselves and others. An emotionally stable adult of any age, gender, or sexual preference who wants to enter into a healthy relationship with another human being would benefit from *Elemental Love Styles*. The book is not for people in dysfunctional, abusive relationships.

Elemental Love Styles is a process of self-discovery divided into four parts.

Part I is where you will learn about the elements and your elemental style, which you'll identify through an Elemental Style Quiz.

Part II is about intimacy and the universal quest for closeness. It looks at how to create a happier, healthier relationship and provides intimacy skills to make it easier to work through problem areas with your partner.

Part III allows you to compare your elemental style to your partner's and identify your greatest strengths and challenges as a couple.

Part IV is where you'll learn how greater self-discovery and intimacy in a relationship can help you achieve your highest potential as an individual.

Introduction

Elemental Love Styles is designed as a guided journey of discovery, so you can feel safe to learn more about yourself and how you relate to a romantic partner.

I wish you many blessings and much happiness during your own journey toward love, and I offer you this book as a guide to help you find your way.

Part 1

Your Elemental Style

1
The Elements: Outside and Inside

For thousands of years, people have tried to understand the world by observing nature and drawing conclusions based on these observations. Many ancient Western philosophies, classical sciences, and spiritual practices are based on the conclusion that the world is made up of four basic elements: fire, air, water, and earth. These elements represent certain aspects of nature and, as the building blocks of creation, make up everything we know. Today the elements still offer a profound way to explain the world, as well as the people who inhabit it.

Not That Kind of Chemistry

First off, I'm not speaking of the elements as they're found in modern chemistry. Instead, I'm referring to the four elements—fire, air, water, and earth—as expressed in the natural world and classical systems of thought.

What Is an Element?

An element is a basic substance complete unto itself. So rather than divide the elements into molecular components, we will define each element as consisting only of itself.

Fire is only fire.
Air is only air.
Water is only water.
Earth is only earth.

While the elements remain complete unto themselves, they also combine with each other to form everything in the world. As an example, let's look at a glass of wine. Since the wine flows as a liquid, you might categorize it as water. But the wine is made of grapes, which come from the earth. To this, add the fire and air of distillation. So while wine primarily consists of water, it would not be such a complex brew without the other elements!

Cheers!

The elements describe every aspect of nature. They are in life. They are every part of life. They are in the world around us, from what we see, to the weather, to the behavior of our fellow man. Anything you see or think about falls within the elemental framework. Because the elements resonate in so many ways—including the way people interact—they can offer insight into the dynamics of human relationships.

Living in the Elements

People use the expression "going out in the elements" to mean "going outside," particularly in rain, snow, or extreme weather. It usually takes a deluge or a blizzard—or some other exaggerated conditions—before we notice the elemental nature of life. But whether we notice them or not, the elements are there all along.

We go out in the elements every day. Most of the time, the elements treat us kindly. The sun is warm rather than roasting. The wind is refreshing rather than roaring. The rain is gentle rather than torrential. And the earth is stable rather than shaking. When they're on their best behavior, we enjoy the elements and might even take them for granted. It is only when the elements act out their harsher qualities that we really pay attention and begin to feel aggravated.

The Elements and Human Personality

Since ancient times, people have theorized about ways to categorize the human personality. While different systems of thought expound different ideas, most have something in common. From the philosophers of Greece to modern psychoanalytic theorists, many great minds have agreed that human personalities come in four types. While each referred to the four personality types by different names, the basic idea is the same. Grouping personalities into four types allows those who study human behavior to better understand how people operate in the world and in relationships with one another.

Personality type: A group of traits, characteristics, behaviors, attitudes, or attributes that represents a specific personality pattern
Elemental psychology: A way of categorizing personality types according to the elements

What Is Elemental Psychology?

Elemental psychology studies the correspondence between human personality and the elements. In other words, the elements outside us symbolize what's inside us. When I call somebody an Earth style, I don't literally mean that he or she is like dirt. Instead, I'm referring to how the individual's inner qualities reflect the outer attributes found in nature.

As an element, Earth is stable and solid; therefore, so is the Earth-style person. Fire is hot and intense, and Fire-style people are warm and inviting. As you will discover, both the Air-style and Water-style personalities also equate to their respective elements.

What Are the Elemental Styles?

Each person is a reflection of the elements found in nature. Because the elements exist inside us as well as outside us, we don't just go out in the elements; we live in them. They are a part of us.

We will explore the elemental styles more thoroughly in upcoming chapters, but here are a few basic traits about each type:

Fire style: Creative and enthusiastic
Air style: Communicative and social
Water style: Emotional and intuitive
Earth style: Practical and grounded

These four elemental styles represent the core human personality types. You will see characteristics from all elements within yourself, but one or two types will be more apparent in your personality. Just as the earlier example of wine mostly resembles water, so, too, one element usually predominates in an individual.

I refer to the predominating element in your personality as your default element. To live in the world, you will rely primarily on this element. The default element shades and directs your relationships and acts as the lens through which you view your experiences.

In this book, I hope to create a picture of each elemental type, not as a static or one-dimensional image but as a set of personality characteristics that make up a complex individual. Elemental categories aren't intended to simplify you but to make it easier for you to understand yourself. They are designed as a guide for self-knowledge.

Your elemental style causes you to develop likes and dislikes and a whole manner of living. It also influences how you operate in relationships and comes with its own set of deeper needs. By understanding each element's deeper needs, you will gain insight into your relationship with your partner as well as with your friends, family members, and co-workers.

An Elemental Beach Party

Four friends of different elemental styles decide to hang out and have some fun. After talking it over for a minute, Fire suggests that they go to the beach. Fire knows the best beach and the fastest way to get there. Air interjects that to ensure a good time, they really should get a map, a few magazines, and the newspaper with the comics and crossword. Water suggests the coolest music to bring and explains where to set up the blankets for the best view of the sunset. Earth checks to make sure they have enough to eat and drink and plenty of sunscreen to go around. Together, the four elemental types make a perfect team and know how to throw the perfect elemental beach party!

All Styles Included Here

Anyone, man or woman, can be any elemental style. While each elemental style comes with a set of specific characteristics, some characteristics show up in all elemental styles.

All the elemental styles can be sexy, attractive, funny, intelligent, or wealthy. In addition to belonging to either gender, these characteristics are not exclusive to any one element. Just as all styles can act angry or hurtful, all styles can love; the differences are in the way each style shows love, anger, hurt, humor, and other parts of the personality.

All styles can be intelligent. Some styles are bold, others talkative; some styles are imaginative and others are organized. The different elemental styles become more clearly defined as we examine how each style expresses universal traits.

Elemental Styles and Your Deeper Needs

Elemental psychology offers its most powerful insights into human personality by defining the deeper needs of each elemental type. Ordinarily, people lack perspective about what they need because they are entrenched in habitual ways of seeing themselves and the world. But elemental psychology can help us cut through these established patterns and gain greater awareness of our relationships and ourselves.

When you chase after false needs,
it is virtually impossible to find happiness.

External influences, such as family members, friends, and even the media, often tell us what types of relationships to pursue. They say our fulfillment depends on finding someone with money, high social status, or good looks. More than likely, though, these external influences promote false needs that won't create happiness in a relationship. Still, you may mistake these false needs for your deeper needs. But these superficial needs will never satisfy your deepest longings.

Separating your real needs from the needs you are told to have is difficult. You may find that you get into patterns when it comes to relationships, always ending up with the same kind of partner, yet never understanding why it doesn't work out. Your belief about whose right for you and how to work things out is deeply ingrained. So perhaps it's time to look at relationships differently.

When you chase after false needs, it is virtually impossible to find happiness. You will only find happiness in a relationship if you're pursuing your true needs—the deeper needs of your elemental type.

Particular Needs Are Something Else

I want to clarify something about deeper needs. You may feel a strong need to live in the country, marry someone of the same religion, or desire other things particular to you. But these particular needs, such as establishing a relationship with someone who loves dogs, do not reflect any specific elemental type; they are your own particular needs. Any element can enjoy certain kinds of movies or music. So if you have a strong need for someone who can dance the salsa—well, that's not about your elemental style or your deeper needs for love. It's particular to you, and that's fine!

Your realness is what attracts a potential partner to you.

I often find that people create lists of particular needs when they are looking for love. Their partner should like sushi and the outdoors, or jazz and baseball. They think that similar interests will make for a lasting relationship. Somehow, they are convinced that someone of a specific height, with a specific amount of body hair, a similar hobby, and/or a specific job will be just right for them. But then that doesn't seem to work either.

Compatibility may be more about whether you and your partner can meet each other's needs, and less about if you both like golf.

While particular needs are important, they don't bring about a successful relationship. The only way you will enjoy a truly fulfilling relationship is to find someone who meets your deeper needs for love. While some particular needs are valid and nonnegotiable, such as the need to date a nonsmoker, don't make your list of particular needs too restrictive. In the end, your particular needs could separate you from someone to love.

Self-Understanding and the Elemental View

When you learn about your elemental style, you'll have a new foundation for understanding yourself. There's a reason why "Know Thyself" was inscribed over the main entrance of the Temple of Apollo at Delphi. Self-understanding is the first, and most important, step toward happiness. Knowing yourself, both the good and the bad parts, and remaining honest about it all creates space for the real you.

Self-understanding is the first, and most important,
step toward happiness.

Essentially, we are all on the same road. We all want love in our lives. We want to be loved and we want to love someone else. What stands in our way of that union is our ability to accept others and ourselves. By using the elements as a model for self-understanding, the possibility for acceptance increases. We don't need to strive for a perfect picture of some unattainable self. We don't need to place our perspective partners in that same box, judging them for their flaws because we cannot accept our own. We can simply be who we are—

works in progress—individuals attempting to grow and make better choices. Even the smallest effort to look at ourselves and grow is a choice toward being real.

Your realness is what attracts a potential partner to you. When you're real, you're authentic. You become your genuine self when you know who you are, and that creates a foundation for success. I hope that exploring your elemental type and learning more about yourself brings you closer to finding, creating, and maintaining a healthy, honest, and truly loving relationship. I know it did for me.

2
Finding Your
Elemental Style

What is your elemental style? You may already think you know after reading chapter 1, but you can find out for sure by completing the following questionnaire. When answering the questions in the Elemental Style Quiz, please keep a few things in mind:

First, there are no right answers. All answers are good; none are better than the others. The answers you pick will be the right answer for you.

Second, answer honestly. To make the most of this questionnaire and gain more personal insight, choose answers that reflect how you really see yourself, rather than how you'd like to see yourself.

If several answers seem equally true, pick the one you feel most strongly about or the one that first jumps out at you.

When answering questions about yourself, always listen to your gut. Thinking too long about how to answer a question only muddies the truth.

After completing the questionnaire, you'll count your responses and learn your elemental style. The four elemental styles are not based on astrology or any other method of defining personality. As you'll see in the upcoming chapters, your elemental style offers a complete picture of you as a complex individual.

You might ask, "Do I have to be just one?" The answer's no! You will see many qualities from all the elements within yourself. The value here is to know which element is the strongest in your personality. That element is the lens you view the world through. It's your default element, the style you will fall back on when you're being most true to yourself and when you're coping with life's troubles. That's your elemental style!

So have fun with this. The questionnaire gives you an opportunity to think about yourself and discover your elemental style. This knowledge will bring you one step closer to understanding your deeper needs for love and creating a fantastic relationship!

Elemental Style Quiz

1. **I see myself primarily as**
   A. Creative, passionate, assertive
   B. Talkative, energetic, independent
   C. Emotional, imaginative, intuitive
   D. Practical, dependable, realistic

2. **My motto would be**
   A. No guts, no glory.
   B. It's all good.
   C. Music calms the savage beast.
   D. An ounce of prevention is worth a pound of cure.

3. **I prefer to wear clothes that are**
   A. Bold and colorful

B. Cool and sharp

C. Comfortable and reflect my mood

D. Conservative and low-key

4. **If I went to a party with a blemish on my face, I would**

A. Hate it

B. Make light of it

C. Try to hide it

D. Ignore it

5. **Where my money is concerned, I**

A. Spend it effortlessly

B. Lose track of it

C. Fluctuate between worry and hope

D. Save it diligently

6. **In life, I most value**

A. Creativity

B. Communication

C. Emotion

D. Security

7. **When it comes to trying new things, I am**

A. Concerned about succeeding

B. Always trying new things

C. Open and receptive

D. Careful and dedicated

8. **When under stress, I can be**

A. Aggressive and abrupt

B. Dismissive and flighty

C. Hypersensitive and moody

D. Rigid and stubborn

9. **When I converse with someone, I am usually the**
   A. Outgoing one
   B. Chatty one
   C. Sensitive one
   D. Sensible one

10. **"Funny" to me is**
    A. Sharp and rapid
    B. Slapstick and witty
    C. Dry and sarcastic
    D. Your basic potty humor

11. **If I were a book, I would be**
    A. Action/adventure
    B. Comedy
    C. Romance/drama
    D. How-to/do-it-yourself

12. **My connection with others is**
    A. Enthusiastic
    B. Verbal
    C. Feelings-based
    D. Tangible/material

13. **I need my home to be a**
    A. Place of pride
    B. Social center
    C. Retreat or escape
    D. Place of beauty and comfort

14. **Feelings for me are**
    A. Explosive and large

B. Light and easy

C. Deep and intense

D. Grounded and metered

15. If I were doing a household task and got interrupted, I would

A. Pick up where I left off, if I thought it was important

B. Forget about it, because I'm doing ten things at once anyway

C. Get a bit flustered with switching gears

D. Go back to it ASAP; I feel uncomfortable when things are left unfinished

16. I would most like to

A. Design something

B. Write something

C. Paint something

D. Build something

17. When I meet a new person, I can be

A. Direct

B. Funny

C. Sensitive

D. Serious

18. If I were a game, I would be

A. Charades

B. Trivial Pursuit

C. Clue

D. Monopoly

19. I really enjoy

A. Roller coasters

B. Comedy clubs

C. Music venues

D. Fine dining

20. **At work, I am a(n)**

A. Leader

B. Mediator

C. Caregiver

D. Organizer

21. **I like my job to offer me**

A. A place to shine

B. Interaction with others

C. Emotional fulfillment

D. A good reputation

22. **I can help others most by offering**

A. Motivation

B. Humor

C. Empathy

D. Assistance

23. **When I think of fairness or justice, I think of my**

A. Big forgiving nature

B. Strong sense of logic

C. Compassionate feelings

D. Checkbook

24. **If life is about give and take, I'm most likely to give a _____ and take a _____.**

A. Big idea/bow

B. Party/"Get Out of Jail Free" card

C. Sympathetic ear/hug

D. Helpful solution/promotion

25. **I often look for a romantic partner who offers**
    A. Admiration
    B. Intelligence
    C. Comfort
    D. Security

26. **I could stand to be a little less**
    A. Boastful
    B. Scattered
    C. Cynical
    D. Uptight

27. **If I loaned a friend twenty dollars and wanted it back, I would**
    A. Ask for it
    B. Forget about it
    C. Feel guilty
    D. Charge interest

28. **Good sex is**
    A. Hot, hot, hot
    B. Cyber
    C. All-consuming
    D. Kicking back and enjoying the attention

29. **At a funeral, I would comfort others by**
    A. Acting as a positive presence
    B. Lightening things up with stories or humor
    C. Consoling and then crying along
    D. Cooking, arranging flowers, and/or carrying the casket

30. **Sharing is**
    A. Not always easy; what's mine is mine
    B. Cool, as long as it doesn't infringe on my freedom
    C. The essence of my approach to life; it makes me happy
    D. Easy; it just works well for me

31. **My personal philosophy is**
    A. No pain, no gain.
    B. Don't worry, be happy.
    C. Love is all there is.
    D. Waste not, want not.

32. **For fun I would choose**
    A. Something active
    B. Crossword puzzles or reading
    C. An art project
    D. Repairing/remodeling something

33. **My vacation would likely include**
    A. Athletics or gambling
    B. Museums or socializing
    C. Theater, music, or movies
    D. Relaxing or pampering

34. **My career allows me to**
    A. Take charge and initiate projects
    B. Exchange ideas and write/teach
    C. Troubleshoot and effect change
    D. Organize details and make money

35. **I like others to think of me as**
    A. Popular

B. Friendly

C. Caring

D. Successful

36. If someone I cared about had a bad impression of me, I would

A. Probably think it was the other person's problem

B. Want to talk it over

C. Feel badly and blame myself

D. Do whatever it takes to reestablish the other person's good opinion of me

37. With friends, I

A. Take charge and make plans

B. Love to just hang out and catch up

C. Listen to their problems and give advice

D. Order in a meal to share while watching a movie

38. If I joined a group, it would be

A. Outdoor adventure

B. Social

C. Therapeutic

D. Philanthropic/political

39. Collectively, I think the world could use more

A. Excitement

B. Laughter

C. Compassion

D. Safety

40. People think I am

A. Creative

B. Talkative

C. Sensitive

D. Responsible

41. I'm afraid of being

    A. Ridiculed

    B. Boring

    C. Unhappy

    D. Imperfect

42. When I dream at night, I am often

    A. Important

    B. Free

    C. Loved

    D. Comfortable

43. If I were an artist, I would be

    A. An actor or rock star

    B. An author or comedian

    C. A poet or painter

    D. A sculptor or architect

44. I am

    A. Memorable

    B. Flexible

    C. Perceptive

    D. Substantive

After completing the questions,
count the number of A, B, C, and D answers and insert
the numbers into the chart on the following page.

ANSWERS/ ELEMENTAL STYLE	YOUR ANSWERS (Insert total number)	YOUR ELEMENTAL STYLE (Rank the elemental style from highest to lowest)
"A" answers: Fire		
"B" answers: Air		
"C" answers: Water		
"D" answers: Earth		
Total:	**44**	

Interpreting Your Results

When looking at the results of your quiz, it is important to keep in mind that everyone, to some degree, is a blend of the elements. All people have a passionate, intellectual, emotional, and practical nature. So even if you score 0 for one of the elemental qualities, this does not mean quality is absent in your personality. It simply means that you lean more strongly toward the other types.

Since we are all a blend of the elements, your results should be viewed as a mix rather than a static value. I think of it as pancake mix—you know, where the recipe says to add more flour for thicker pancakes or add more milk for thinner pancakes. It doesn't give a specific amount to add or subtract—just less or more. For this reason, I am going to divide the results into four categories without assigning numeric scores:

Standing Out: One element predominates.
Dynamic Duo: Two elements share a close score.
Three's a Charm: Three elements score about even.
Bases Covered: All four elements are about equal.

Standing Out: One element predominates

When one element is the strong leader of the elemental types in your score, you are rarely surprised. You are pretty clear that you often operate from a singular elemental place, and that element is familiar to you.

Discovering how to make the most of your element is more defined and specific. However, the chance that the negative aspects of your element are strong in your personality is greater. Care should be taken to thoroughly review all the qualities of your singular elemental approach. This gives you the opportunity to perfect your element and avoid elemental irritation.

Dynamic Duo: Two elements share a close score

Two elements of near equal importance is the most common combination for elemental types. Both work with each other to create an elemental combo. You may find that one of the pair scored higher than the other. You may even recognize one more strongly than the other. The purpose of finding out your element is to become more aware.

One woman's response to the quiz was that she knew she had Air quality in her character, but finding out that she also had strong Water qualities explained so much about certain actions and behaviors she hadn't given space for in herself. For her, the Water qualities had felt wrong. She judged them. They didn't fit with her self-image, but then she found out that they could.

By seeing the two-element combination as a pair of elemental qualities, you get the benefit of unified strengths. It can also help with the negative sides of both. One element may modify or buffer the darker side of the other. This can soften the harsher side and make finding your elemental potential easier.

Three's a Charm: Three elements score about even

Here you have three elements that score relatively the same and one element that scores obviously less. This combination is multi-faceted, and the range of actions and behaviors that you operate from is wider.

There is a tendency with three strong elements to be capable of interacting easily within many groups of people. Three is dynamic, and it creates a movement of energy from one element to the other.

As with the two-element score, there is likely to still be one element that stands out. That's the element you are most familiar with and conscious of. By allowing yourself to see the bigger picture, you gain insight into strengths you might not recognize.

The difficulty with the three-element type actually lies with the weaker element. Many people with this combination will find that they are attracted to someone who has a strong placement of their missing element. While this can work out well, it can also make it hard to see if their partner is operating from his or her best self in the relationship.

Bases Covered: All four elements are about equal

When the four elements are equal, you have access to the most varied interactions with yourself. The person with this combination can reach into his or her personality and find their passion, intellect, emotions, and practicality more easily. The interaction is more harmonious and being "good" at a number of things comes more readily.

Again, one element may stand out more, and that would be the best place to start when identifying with an elemental type. However, it is fine to be elementally equal. Perhaps you could say, "I'm strong in all four, but I lean toward Air." That still gives you an elemental style, but you connect with all the styles.

The issue to look at for the equal-four combination is one of stasis. Take care to look at the elemental qualities and discover which inner growth work seems most important for you. This combination can be so solid and complex. Don't allow the evenness to create a jack-of-all-trades, master-of-none scenario. We all need friction to reveal the deeper layers.

Remember, we are not cookie cutters.
While we seek to find out more about ourselves,
we are dynamic first and quantified second.

Overview

The element with the highest number of answers is your primary elemental style. Remember, you can be a combination of two, three, or all four elemental styles. It is perfectly acceptable and fairly common to be a Fire/Air, Water/Air, or any other combination. By working with your style, you will be able to see how and when certain elemental qualities in your personality emerge. For example, I test as a Fire/Water: strongest for Fire, followed closely by Water. I see strong Fire qualities when I'm dealing with my lover, friends, and family, but I am very clearly Water in my professional practice, and then Watery when needed with my lover, friends, and family. Remember, we are not cookie cutters. While we seek to find out more about ourselves, we are dynamic first and quantified second.

The quiz is designed to help you with self-reflection. It is not meant to be absolute. It is a pointer and was written to provide you with direction. Personality is complex, so allow your discovery to have flexibility. The element that you connect with in the present may take on new dimensions as you understand your needs more completely. Most of us will lean toward one element. At least in our hearts we will see ourselves in a particular way.

Most of us will lean toward one element. At least in our hearts we will see ourselves a particular way. That's where you should begin and that's the elemental style you can now read about in chapters 3 (Fire), 4 (Air), 5 (Water), or 6 (Earth).

3
Fire Style: Creative

Hear ye! Hear ye! Let a proclamation go forth that reads,
"It shall be known throughout the land: There is no other
more expressive or creative than Fire."

Think about the last time you got really excited about an important happening in your life. That excitement is the element of Fire within you. Fire-style people live in that excitement. Their whole way of being is focused on enthusiasm, energy, and willfulness. The power to create makes Fire people bold and innovative.

The four fictional characters that follow represent the energy of Fire. They were chosen to show the variety in Fire's style. Because they are characters from our cultural mainstream, I like to think of them as the Fire we know.

Wonder Woman

Descended from royalty, Wonder Woman is a great Fire-style character from the world of comics. With her megawarrior persona, she is a take-charge individual: direct, resourceful, and fearless. For women, she represents empowerment; for everyone, she shows the absolute conviction that results when we're filled with the passion of Fire.

Wonder Woman exudes strength. She can compete with her male counterparts, human and superhero alike, and stands as a role model for determination and courage. As a Fire, Wonder Woman is forceful, but, first and foremost, she uses that force to achieve positive results. Both kind and noble, she's a royal superhero who hasn't lost her everyday touch.

The Fonz

This is one of my favorite picks for Fire. Fonzie, played by Henry Winkler in *Happy Days*, is sure of himself on every level. As the leader of the pack, "I'm wrong" doesn't show up in his vocabulary. The very notion of him messing up is unthinkable. How Fire!

The Fonz is also self-possessed and self-confident. I suppose you're getting the picture that Fire is about the self. But it's not in the negative way customarily associated with selfish. Confidence is part of Fire's trademark style, and Fonzie is his own biggest fan. Why not? Every time he looks in the mirror, he has to smile and say, "Aaay." The Fonz knows he's perfection.

James Bond

Self-confident without appearing brash, James Bond is charming and passionate. People find Bond exciting, and he is well aware of his magnetic power. He's a trendsetter, blazing with originality in everything, from the way he dresses to the way he undresses. Even though he's a spy, he wouldn't think of going incognito. With his jazzy clothes and flashy car, he's not afraid of attention.

His innovative style shows through in his exploits both in and out of the bedroom. James Bond has mastered creative thinking, and Fire is the creativity king. He does everything in a big way. From his har-rowing escape methods to his charismatic effect on the ladies, James Bond is hot!

Maude

Played by Bea Arthur on TV, Maude verges on a caricature of extro-verted confidence. Perhaps we love her because she calls it as she sees it, offering refreshing frankness that we'd love to find in real life. Maude is opinionated and makes us laugh because her insights are so spot-on. If I wanted someone to break it all down for me, I'd pick Maude.

Consistent with Fire style, Maude is outspoken and usually gets the last word. She's a risk taker and a fearless one at that. Willing to take a stand on controversial topics, she defies any element she con-siders oppressive. Above all, Fire style is about passion.

The Fire You Are

Good Morning, Fire

Off to a rip-roaring start, your day is a creative blast from the moment your eyes sense the dawn. Whether you're jumping out of bed or taking a bit of a stretch, you are already thinking about what to do with the day. From the moment you wake up, ideas start popping into your head. How are you ever going to put it all into action? It seems that every aspect of your life—career, home, social life, and hobbies—wants your energy and attention. Good thing you've got more than enough stamina to go around!

Fire is motivated to excel. You will push yourself from the moment you get up. Why not start the day with a workout, portfolio strategy, or tennis set? You can get yourself charged up while planning your next getaway, probably to some best-kept-secret discovery. Every day is interesting and exciting—a potpourri of creative opportunity—and you settle for nothing less.

Even when you're in a hurry, you make time to take care of yourself. You are special, and you treat yourself accordingly. In the shower, the temperature has to be just right; the shampoo and soap, what you consider the best brands; the towels or robe, the quality you deserve. You know what's good, and what's good is good for you.

Your closet is a showcase of fashion and style—not one style in particular, but *your* style. Everything looks as if it were designed with you in mind. Expression is a strong suit for Fire, so your look is a great place to learn what you're all about. And you look great! As you check yourself in the mirror, you're not surprised; you still look great!

Heading out to the kitchen, breakfast may be on the run, but it's the finest. So even if you're grabbing a banana on your way out the door, it's the best banana in the bunch! You leave the house ready to impress us all. People admire Fire, and you admire yourself. You've got a style that's all your own, and you know it!

When We First Meet Fire

Fire loves an audience, and meeting new people gives you a stage. From the moment you walk into a room, you're the center of attention. Instinctively drawn to your positive energy and enthusiasm, people find you compelling. It's your warmth and charm that cast the spell. Others gather around to feel the glow and get inspired.

When meeting you, we can expect a whole lot more than a handshake. You offer a warm smile and a deep, knowing look. You reach out, lean forward, and make people believe you've been dying to meet them.

You radiate excitement, and people think, "Who's that?" as soon as they spot you. You're bold about making new connections; your upbeat attitude melts the heart of even the coolest customer. Why, people feel happier just standing next to you.

High energy and confidence mix for a mighty powerful combination. You retain the power of youth—which keeps the twinkle in your eye and the lightness in your heart no matter what your age. A true original, you always leave a lasting impression.

Talk to Me, Fire

When you speak, people listen. Perhaps your commanding tone directs attention your way. Perhaps it's that ever-present confidence. Either way, people want to hear you, not only for what you're saying but also for the original way you express yourself. You have flair and dramatize your words with gestures and facial expressions. Your lively manner helps listeners see what you see, and your enthusiasm makes the world far more colorful. Thank goodness we have you!

When you speak, it's with passion and conviction, giving you great appeal no matter what you're discussing. You're captivating and hold listeners spellbound! When you tell a simple anecdote, it often becomes a compelling epic drama. Fire knows how to tell a story, and people gather to hear your tales.

You are confident about your many opinions and strong beliefs. On top of that, you love getting others to see things your way. Passionate about what you believe, you adore making grand pronouncements. Certainly you are no stranger to exaggeration. After all, bigger is better, right?

Fire, you're the one who will tell us about the best doctor in town, the worst restaurant, the most expensive bottle of wine, and the cheapest place to buy gas. If it isn't big, bold, and important, it isn't worth saying. Unless you find the conversation significant, you're bored silly. Feeding off life's excitement, you have little patience for the details. Cut to the chase and give you the brilliant part, because that's all you want to hear. Talking with Fire leaves many in awe, and they're sure to come back for more.

Playing with Fire

Fire loves to play, and you play to win. Fiercely competitive, you can be friendly, but a truly friendly game? Now, that's another thing altogether. That's because you approach competition as if the fate of the world hangs in the balance, and, well, it does—your world, anyway. So whether you're playing golf, volleyball, or cards, winning represents a point of personal pride for you.

With a constant need to prove yourself, sports, games, and dares are the ideal place for you to show off. You're the person who says, "Oh yeah? I'll show you!" However, if Fire loses fair and square, which rarely happens, you will graciously concede. The other person must have been really good, or else you were having a bad day. Anyway, a loss provides an incentive for you to put in more practice. You'll trounce them next time, that's for sure!

A challenge in just about any arena is fun for you, and your range is quite wide. You might go skiing one weekend to see who makes it to the bottom first. A few weeks later, you're playing high-stakes backgammon with friends. All in fun, but you still play for keeps. Your approach is to take no prisoners and show no mercy, but whatever happens, your positive outlook makes you the winner, and you're sure of that.

Fire Helps Out

Anyone would say you are generous and thoughtful. You love to serve others and feel good about giving your time and money. For Fire, it's about duty. The less fortunate bring out your charitable nature. You're the first to volunteer during an emergency, and your leadership and vision motivate others to follow your example. You are the definition of grace under pressure, bringing order and calm, even during trying times.

Your generosity and thoughtfulness extend to everyone you know. By remembering special occasions, sending cards, or making calls, you show someone that you care. You also have a knack for gift giving, picking the perfect present, and making every event memorable.

Fire really shows its noble side by encouraging others to do their best. A natural cheerleader, you bolster and motivate people. After a long day of helping someone move, Fire will turn to a group of friends and say, "Just a few more boxes. We're doing great! We can finish it and then grab that pizza and feel really good about all this!" Fire never quits, and that is often the greatest help of all!

Teaming Up with Fire

Fire has an independent spirit, so you usually like to go it alone. But you're also a natural-born leader and will partner with someone as long as you're in charge. After all, you are the star! People let you call the shots because you work hard and lead by example.

Once on a team, Fire usually steps in and takes command. You have the vision and know how a project should unfold. Others have talent and creativity, and you're right there with praise and encouragement; but, by golly, you're the top dog. When decisions have to be made, you'll make them. You're not a dictator—you know better than that, but trying to curb your bossy tendencies wouldn't hurt, either.

With you leading the way, your teammates gain abundant ideas, creative approaches, and dynamic solutions. You are a huge asset to any group, and your winning consciousness illuminates the team. Whether in sports or sales or during an election, you know how to bring home the victory!

Fanning the Flames with Fire

The room blazes with aromatic candles. Sultry music simmers in the background. Chocolates melt and a champagne cork explodes. Fire, you are hot! Romantic to your very core, you love to set the stage for seduction, and setting the stage is so much of the fun! You exude sexuality and know how to turn up the heat and burn up the sheets. Take your time. Why rush when it's so exciting to get your partner in the mood?

For Fire, sex is more than a physical experience. You want to share yourself, body and soul. You're turned on just looking in your lover's eyes, and the lights are definitely on so you can see and be seen. Sex for you is about expressing yourself, so you jump in and abandon yourself to desire.

With your creativity and stamina, you make each encounter different and memorable. Your repertoire includes countless ways to ignite your lover's passion. You invent new positions and explore every inch of your partner, not to mention the house or even the yard!

Sounds like fun, right? Well, that's a big part of the experience. With you, sex is never routine, never predictable. All this variety keeps it spicy and keeps your lover wanting more.

As long as your partner can show you and tell you how amazing you are in the bedroom department, you're happy. When you feel adored and appreciated, the creativity, the passion, and the love keep on coming strong.

Fire in the World

Wherever you find yourself, you are a superstar! Fire thrives in the spotlight and loves to take center stage. Drawn to occupations where your brilliance gets a chance to shine, you feel at home with an audience. Whether in the courtroom, theater, or arena, you create a sensation. As a lawyer in front of the jury or a parent in front of the kids, you love to put on a display, command attention, and give the crowd a good time.

You enjoy the big paycheck, status, and renown, but you need to know you're making a difference. Fire strives for more than position; you want to have an impact. With a position of authority, you can bring your ideas to fruition and create significant change.

Entrepreneur extraordinaire—that's Fire, and a natural leader too. You're enterprising, motivated, and a risk taker. You believe in your ideas, and why not? They're ingenious. You have so much faith in what you're doing that help comes easily. On the job, people line up and sign up for your projects. In whatever career you pursue, your star power and confident Fire-style persistence raise you to the top.

Fire as a Friend

Outgoing and positive, Fire people make friends easily, and they also make great friends. You know how to have fun! Always up for something new, you make everyday excursions feel like world-class adventures. You keep your friends laughing with your stories and antics, and you're always the one who catches the really big fish. Sure, you may embellish a bit, but people love to hear about your adventures and listen wide-eyed to every twist and turn.

Popular without even trying, you make people feel good and know how to have a good time. Even when you're having fun, you inspire and motivate. One Fire friend of mine always—and I mean always—has a positive word to say. No matter what the circumstances, he convinces me I can do it. What a great friend!

With your open heart and open checkbook, you're always there for people. Friends gather around as if you're a roaring campfire and bask in your warmth and glow. Whether you're helping someone move, get a job, or find a soul mate, you do everything with a smile, a pat on the back, and words of encouragement. Even in a disagreement, you're the one with forgiveness in mind. When I'm thinking good vibrations, I'm thinking of you!

At Home with Fire

Whether you live in a tiny apartment or a spacious house, your home radiates originality. It expresses *you*, through and through. Big, bold, original—that's Fire's style, and your living space reflects it. You know how to add that special zing to make the place sing! Mixing pieces from different eras, you create an exciting mix all your own. Put a lava lamp on a Victorian table? You have the confidence to pull it off.

Burning with ideas, you're ready, willing, and able to try something new. Why settle for the same old, same old when you can get rid of this, bring in that, move this around, and—voila!—a dazzling new look! You can turn boards and bricks into bookcases, sheets and saris into window treatments, and stones and twigs into centerpieces. You're a nonconformist with the courage to create a one-of-a-kind home environment.

Lighting reigns supreme for Fire. It creates the mood, sets the tone, makes the house a home, and gives your place that special radiance. There's a warm glow in the living room, a cheery sparkle in the kitchen, and a sexy twinkle in the bedroom. So whether bright or dim, the lighting is designed to satisfy you. Sure, you've got your own radiant glow, but the right lighting never hurts.

Ultimately, you view your living space the way an artist sees a canvas. Your place functions as a blank slate where you can explore your ideas, display your creativity, and feel proud. For you, home becomes a statement, a proclamation of your creative vision and genius.

Be Fire's Guest

Fire, you are the original party animal! For you, a party means an audience, and that represents a chance to show people a stellar time.

You know how to throw a unique, unforgettable bash, wowing your guests and taking your place in the spotlight.

Put a new spin on a traditional holiday? You bet you will! Instead of a Christmas party, you might host a Sinatra birthday bash with an old-school cocktail party and Frank's carols playing on the sound system. Originality means everything to you, so you strive to do what's never been done and give your guests something to talk about for weeks to come.

When you invite people to your place, they can count on the hottest ticket in town. At your party, everything dazzles—from the eclectic guest list and novel décor to the distinctive food and avant-garde music. Only the best, the most interesting, and the most vibrant will do.

Charismatic and charming, you know how to captivate your crowd. You hold court, gliding graciously from group to group, making sure that everybody, including yourself, is having one hell of a great time.

When the party gets going, where are you? Center stage! You're the bringer of this good time. You bask in the attention and love to hear people say they're having a blast. Big memories and accolades like this are partly why you threw the party in the first place. In fact, you might be getting ready to sing one of Frank's tunes yourself. "My Way," anyone?

Fire's Deeper Needs

Fire, you're a big personality. You're creative, original, generous, and competitive. But what you want most in the world is for other people to recognize just how special you are, and to let you know how much they appreciate your big ideas. After all, your creativity and vision are what make life so much fun.

With Fire, nothing dignifies like grandeur. People can't tell you often enough or in big enough ways how wonderful you are. You've got greatness written all over you, and we know it!

The Deeper Needs of Fire

- Having space to take charge and create
- Feeling a sense of importance
- Gaining recognition and praise from others

Fire Outside and Fire Inside

Fire is a symbol for your elemental qualities. The chart below shows and compares how the attributes of fire in nature correspond with these elemental qualities of Fire in your personality.

FIRE IN NATURE ELEMENTAL ATTRIBUTES	YOUR FIERY NATURE ELEMENTAL QUALITIES
Hot	Passionate, enthusiastic, positive, enterprising, motivational, inspiring
Illuminating	Original, creative, innovative, resourceful
Powerful	Confident, bold, extroverted, assertive, take-charge, courageous, energetic, adventurous
Warm	Outgoing, charming, fun-loving, kind, friendly, happy, generous, noble, honest
Intense	Impulsive, ambitious, competitive
Bright	Center of attention, starring role, playful

4
Air Style: Intellectual

an·swer [ʹan(t)-sər]: The correct reply or
solution that Air style has.
Why? Because Air asks all the questions;
that's how they get all the answers!

People spend a lot of time either thinking or talking, and the mind is an intensely active part of living. The thinking part of you represents the Air within you. Air-style people are permeated with thoughts. Their whole way of being is centered on language, information, humor, and curiosity. The power of the word makes Air people precise and truth seeking.

The four fictional characters that follow represent the energy of Air. They were chosen to show the variety in Air's style. Because they are characters from our cultural mainstream, I like to think of them as the Air we know.

Lucy Ricardo

One of the funniest and most endearing characters in television history, Lucy Ricardo, played by Lucille Ball on *I Love Lucy*, has true Air style. Lucy loves to clown around, and she is always more than ready to concoct her next scheme. Air is the comedian of the elemental styles, and Lucy shows us the full range of Air humor. From her hysterical facial expressions to her innocent plays on words, Lucy keeps us laughing.

She is a chatterbox; in fact, she keeps the plotline moving because she is such a good storyteller. Always ready to dramatize a tale, Lucy's mastery of language is a big part of her charm. She sets up her day-to-day life as more than a punch line; she's a full-on comedic routine. What we see in her is Air's range with words, wit, and nonsense; and thank goodness for it, because we all need a laugh.

Luke Skywalker

Eager and heroic, Luke Skywalker, played by Mark Hamill in the *Star Wars* saga, is a perfect picture of impetuous and spirited youth. His alert, decisive, and uninhibited manner reflects his abundant Air qualities. Luke is an independent thinker; he makes up his own mind and does things his own way. He'll even disobey Master Yoda and fly off alone to fight the dark Lord Vader.

Truth and justice motivate him; after all, these principles are the essence of the Jedi. Truth, freedom, and the search for justice are also the foundation of Air style. More deeply, the Jedi way is a quest for harmony and balance, which Luke develops as his character grows along the way. Harmony and balance are, again, essential to the Air view of life.

Alice in Wonderland

"Curiouser and curiouser!" cried Alice. The beloved main character of Lewis Carroll's *Alice in Wonderland* was unquestionably inquisitive! Her curiosity sets the story in motion when she follows the White Rabbit down the hole. After that, it's one experiment after another.

From the tea party to the mushroom tasting, Alice searches for answers; that's a foundation of Air.

Alice's experience, though, is fraught with the silly nonsense she encounters. Wonderland, after all, does not conform to her ordinary world. Alice is logical and would like nothing more than to figure things out. She wants fairness, and most of the time that's not what she finds. Still, her insistence on making sense of it all demonstrates her search for truth, and that makes her one of my favorite Air-style girls.

Clark Kent

As a journalist, Clark Kent is a clear choice for an Air man. The intellectual alter ego of Superman, Clark is intelligent and interested in educating himself. He loves journalism and takes an avid interest in reading and learning. His smarts are not confined to books, though; Clark has a dry sense of humor that he uses with his boss and co-workers. He's observant, and the information he gains increases his mental warehouse of knowledge.

Idealistic and fair-minded, Mr. Kent, as he's known around the office, sees the good in people. He uses his powers, both mental and physical, to preserve law and order. Clark has a soaring need to understand the world and learn the truth. This philosophy, which directs his behavior as a superhero, is a guiding tenet of Air.

The Air You Are

Good Morning, Air

Morning probably starts pretty early for you. Wide awake, alert, and abounding with ideas, Air often catches up on the day long before sunrise. Multitasking is your middle name, so you hit the ground running and start your morning with a flurry of activity. You send emails and text messages, watch the news on TV, listen to the traffic report on the radio, read the newspaper, and flip through a magazine all at the same time! With your ravenous curiosity, there's no such thing as too much information. In fact, you prefer catching up on breaking news to sitting down and eating breakfast. More coffee, anyone?

You quickly prepare for the day. Busy, busy—there's so much to do and no time to waste. After all, a day has only 1,440 minutes, and you have something planned for each one. Even when hurrying, you manage to look sharp and put together. No fashion slave, your eccentric edge and unconventional style set you apart. Your look is clean, crisp, and definite, and you are no stranger to hair gel.

Versatile and fast on your toes, it's amazing how easily you switch gears. If you discover that the shirt you want to wear has a small stain, you pick a new one, pronto. You might even get a chuckle out of it; life has a way of testing your adaptability, and you enjoy the challenge.

Running out the door, you're often late or can't find something; no matter—you've got yourself covered. After all, who else can keep so many things spinning at once and make it look like a breeze?

When We First Meet Air

Curious about everyone and everything, you ask lots of questions. Then you store all the answers in your mental warehouse. That's where you've amassed the facts, figures, and details that make up the database of your mind. With quick recall, your memory makes associations every day because you're always encountering people and situations that remind you of something. "Say, you must be from Chicago," you remark to new company; and, of course, you're correct. That accent is just like your college roommate's. How could you miss?

You find meeting people mentally stimulating. With each new encounter, you learn something interesting. Quick to say, "Wow! That's fascinating," you enjoy creating a wider and wider net of contacts, and each new person adds to your extensive range of knowledge. This allows you to comment on just about anything. I know one Air woman who can talk about classical music, auto repair, and comic books from the '60s with at least a cursory familiarity. Her ease with an array of topics shows that she's not only interested but she's also interesting.

People enjoy your company and laugh a lot when they're with you. A charming storyteller, you know how to captivate your listeners and provide an endless supply of conversational tidbits. You can turn the tale of a flat tire into a sidesplitting farce while managing to fold in some facts about the invention of the wheel, the history of Route 66, and how to get better gas mileage.

Talk to Me, Air

"Can we talk?" Those are some of your favorite words. You love to discuss, debate, dialogue, dish, converse, and chat. As long as words are exchanged, you are in your comfort zone. Well spoken and articulate, you know how to think on your feet and can talk your way into and out of most situations. It reminds me of an Air guy I know who can change the subject of a conversation and you never even know it's happened. Better yet, he can spin the exchange so that the most serious topic leaves you laughing.

It's that kind of witty rapid mind that leaves all topics up for grabs with Air. No subject is off-limits; no minutia is too obscure. With your keen way of balancing knowledge with jest, even the usual taboos of religion and politics are fair game. Since you can see the humor even in difficult situations, people appreciate how you lighten the mood.

You are the quintessential conversationalist. If a friend gets engaged, you can expound on how diamonds are mined in South Africa and add how they're set in Manhattan. At the same time, you will share the word of the day from your favorite information website. You derive great joy from sharing your knowledge because it connects you with other people and creates a more secure social bond.

I think most people love spending time with Air because you are always telling a humorous anecdote, relaying a gut-busting joke, or catching people unawares with your barbs and witty observations. You're so funny that friends warn you, "Please, wait until I'm finished chewing, because I'm afraid I'll die laughing." This might be funny too, if it weren't so serious.

Playing with Air

In most situations, your first instinct is to form a social group and establish a sense of community. You love to bring people together in a setting where they can play games, have fun, and engage in discussions. Interaction is like breathing for you, so much so that you can be ready on the spur of the moment to have a good time. If a friend calls, asks you to a movie, and offers to pick you up in five minutes, by the time your ride arrives, you're waiting to pile into the car with four other friends. "The more the merrier" are words you live by.

You see the world through a lens of humor and definitely get the cosmic joke that life is always playing on mere mortals. Able to laugh at yourself and your foibles, you revel in the absurdity of life. You often say things like "The funniest thing happened to me" and "You've got to hear this one." When you run out of gas at midnight on a deserted highway, you can turn the experience into a hilarious tale that will make other people wish they'd been there.

For you, every experience represents a chance for fun. When you choose an activity, it's something stimulating and informative. You tell jokes during open-mike night at a comedy club, participate in a downtown art walk and discussion, or hang out in a bar where five TVs play different programs and five friends discuss different topics. You can take it all in and then some.

To your mind, most people take themselves too seriously, and you love nothing more than to lighten things up. Your motto is "All in good fun," and you can't resist playing good-natured practical jokes or even acting goofy and silly at times. You use humor to create harmony and, as a natural diplomat, understand that nothing breaks the ice like laughter.

Air Helps Out

At every task, you're speedy and zip from thing to thing. While you do a lot of work and do it quickly, you don't cross every *t* and dot every *i*. But, hey, look at how much you accomplish. Meticulous perfectionist? Not you. You're all about getting things done. At a painting party, you'll finish your wall before everyone else, all while fielding phone calls, changing CDs, ordering pizza, and giving everybody news updates. While you're done in no time, you probably got as much paint on yourself as you did on the wall.

Your multitasking talents are legendary, and your depth of knowledge amazes people. You are easily considered a trusted advisor and font of information. Whether the question relates to law, government, education, business, entertainment, or anything else, you either know the answer or know how to find it.

Clear-thinking and logical, you're the go-to person when people need to sort out confusing situations. With wisdom gained through both experience and study, you help others cut through the clutter and see the truth. One of the most objective individuals I know is an Air. People constantly ask for his opinion because he has an independent mind and can offer guidance without judgment.

Air has a sharp-thinking mind, and it gives you the ability to discriminate between the core of an issue and the fluff. You can quickly analyze a situation or problem. To you, what's important just stands out. There would be no use putting homing devices on the chickens when there's a fox in the henhouse.

Teaming Up with Air

People respond to your positive energy and consider you a voice of reason. This makes you a natural for team efforts. Because you're willing to look at all sides of a situation, people see you as fair-minded and open to different viewpoints. You are the impartial colleague, and you bring people together. Nothing makes you happier.

Getting involved in any group enterprise stimulates your eager and inquisitive mind. Different opinions inspire you, and you're the first to say, "Tell me more." You don't even mind if things get heated. Diplomatic and tactful, you know how to handle fragile egos. If people argue, you can smooth their ruffled feathers. Because you understand both points of view, you can suggest a compromise that everyone accepts.

With a knack for diplomacy, you easily resolve conflicts. You're smooth and persuasive and can state your case without alienating fellow team members or coming across as a know-it-all. People enjoy your insights and find your suggestions helpful.

If the team reaches an impasse, you offer the humorous remark that puts everything in perspective, lightens things up, and allows people to move to the next stage. When the team has to make the all-important choice between dueling colas for a holiday party mixer, you'll suggest that it doesn't really matter—as long the event features some smooth bourbon.

Pillow Talk with Air

You're probably not the quietest one in the bedroom. An aficionado of verbal eroticism, you love provocative phone calls, suggestive emails, or just the right word whispered in your ear. "Talk dirty to me, baby" is just the kind of suggestion that gets you in the mood.

Turned on by conversation and mental stimulation, Air will dress up, role-play, and act out scenarios. You want to have fun with your partner and like to keep things on the lighter side, free from heavy emotions. Play baseball locker room? French maid or doctor? Why not run the gamut and play nuns gone wild? Variety is the spice of (sex) life for you, so you're up for anything. You're happy to try new locations, positions, and props. When you get bored mentally, you get turned off physically, so you're more than willing to find new ways to keep the wind in your sails.

Undaunted by headaches, bad backs, or other sexual buzz kills, you can always make things happen. Adaptable and versatile, you try this and try that and can usually get your partner in the mood. Thanks to your lighthearted attitude and flexible approach, you manage to make sex funny and make fun sexy.

Air in the World

Three things—language skills, social interaction, and humor—are what inspire, direct, and guide your choice of career. Language, in spoken and written forms, is essential to Air style. Many of your choices in the work world involve your talent with words. You could have a career as a teacher, journalist, or author or find yourself in advertising, law, or grant writing.

Because you're comfortable speaking extemporaneously as well as bringing people together, you'd make an ideal fundraiser or talk-show personality. One of my favorite Air guys is a gentleman I call the "hospitality king." He manages food and beverage services in major New York hotels. He's responsible for a lot but really soars in the job's social aspects. This guy can troubleshoot a wedding and tactfully convince the father of the bride to come down from the ceiling and cheerfully pay the bill.

Diplomacy and sense of humor are two of your greatest strengths, and you always put them to good use. As a judge or a stand-up comic, you are a clever critic, making your point without turning people off.

Wry, witty, or downright audacious, you can make people laugh and get them thinking.

Air as a Friend

I can't emphasize enough how much of a riot you are. "You crack me up" does not adequately describe the uproarious laughter that erupts whenever you get together with friends. Your mind, and its funny view of things, is so fast. You just keep them coming, one after another, to the point where people's cheeks hurt from laughing so hard.

Beyond your sense of humor, people respect your intelligence and ability to think clearly and often seek your advice and ask your opinion. Since you love to talk and are so well read, you're happy to share your views. People respect your unbiased thoughts and insights and often heed your advice.

You bring variety and different viewpoints into your friends' lives. I can go to the movies with you and discuss the film from many perspectives because you've read so many reviews and are so well informed about related topics. For many activities, you're the ideal companion: fun, flexible, and fascinating.

With your friends, you need things to stay free and loose. You want to maintain your independence, and you value someone who gives you space for your own ideas. You're often the person who's wearing a political button or cause bracelet, fearlessly displaying your beliefs and standing up for what's right.

At Home with Air

"Come right in. Don't be shy. There's plenty of room for one more." A full-on invitation greets us at your house. Air loves company, and your home is set up for conversation and socializing with open spaces, lots of seating, and full media access.

Even when you're at home, you want to stay connected to the world. What could be better than a TV in every room? Well, a telephone and magazine rack next to the toilet come to mind, but, hey, that's probably too much information.

Everything about your place is eclectic. From your mixed styles of décor to the keepsakes and mementos you've picked up during your travels, variety is evident in every room. Books on every topic, magazines, and the latest *TV Guide* are ever-present. Every square inch has something going on. If the bookshelves aren't already packed with books, there's plenty of room for the latest knickknack.

Most of this busy-ness is designed to keep you mentally stimulated and up to date. Current events, from politics to star gossip, fascinate you, and you maintain quite a setup to stay informed. You've conveniently placed a full set of current tech features throughout your home. You can watch TV and DVDs, listen to CDs, send emails, download movies, and play games—all while speaking to your best friend on your new headset!

Be Air's Guest

For you, a get-together doesn't require a holiday or special occasion. Anytime will do for socializing, and you have a long list of folks to hang out with. So inviting people to a party at your place comes naturally. You love to get interesting, informed, articulate people together and watch the conversations take flight. The exchange of ideas really gets you buzzing.

The more diverse the crowd, the better you like it. You thrive on variety and freedom of choice, so you offer the same to your guests. Your bar includes everything imaginable, and you serve lots of distinctive finger food so that people can eat while they're talking and not have to lift a fork.

A pro at setting up connections, you make sure to introduce people with even the most obscure things in common. The history buffs, the photography bugs, and even two guests with the same middle name are all captives to your fantastic recall. By the time people leave your gathering, they've made friends or at least a wonderful new contact.

Laughter is your life's soundtrack, so certainly it is the centerpiece of your party. When people are laughing, the conversations and introductions go all the more smoothly. Light and freewheeling, you might even have slapstick movies playing on the TV with the sound off or have an entertainer who juggles bowling balls just to give everyone an extra laugh.

Air's Deeper Needs

Air, you're a thinker and a communicator. What you want most in the world is freedom and truth. After all, that's what makes your life so invigorating.

With Air, nothing informs like variety. You need the space to stimulate your mind and learn the truth about the world through experience and interactions with other people.

The Deeper Needs of Air

- Unrestricted movement and the quest for truth
- Engaging in social interactions and humor
- Space for mental stimulation

Air Outside and Air Inside

Air is a symbol for your elemental qualities. The chart below shows and compares how the attributes of air in nature correspond with these elemental qualities of Air in your personality.

AIR IN NATURE ELEMENTAL ATTRIBUTES	YOUR AIRY NATURE ELEMENTAL QUALITIES
Clear	Wise, intelligent, fair, astute, persuasive
Breezy	Talkative, articulate, communicative
Refreshing	Funny, humorous, vivacious, versatile
Invigorating	Intellectual, stimulating, curious, eccentric
Crisp	Diplomatic, keen, quick-witted, graceful, sharp
Circulating	Social, group-oriented, popular, animated
Fresh	Adaptable, flexible, independent, alert, freedom-loving

5
Water Style: Emotional

If feelings are a way to see,
then that's how Water wants to be,
'cause logic's not a place to start
when all of life is viewed as art.

Feelings are complex and they often defy logic. Yet our emotions guide us and they draw us toward our heart's desires. The emotional part of you is the element of Water within you. Water-style people are immersed in feelings and sensations. Their whole way of being dissolves in imagination, intuition, and connectedness. The power to feel makes Water people artistic and empathetic.

The four fictional characters that follow represent the energy of Water. They were chosen to show the variety in Water's style. Because they are characters from our cultural mainstream, I like to think of them as the Water we know.

Romeo

In Shakespeare's classic love story *Romeo and Juliet*, from the moment Romeo espies fair Juliet, he pledges his undying devotion.

Romeo's feelings for Juliet take precedence over everything, even family loyalty, because she has opened his heart.

With a name that people equate with "romantic love," Romeo is sensitive, chivalrous, and a bit naive. Before meeting Juliet, he doubts that love will be reciprocated in his life at all. But when he falls in love with Juliet at first sight, Romeo decides to pursue her, regardless of the consequences.

Romeo represents the complex emotional life of Water. From the elation of love to the sadness of separation, Romeo provides a wide-ranging picture of human feelings.

Cinderella

We can all identify with the way Cinderella daydreams about romance, happiness, and a heavenly match. People root for Cinderella because she's good-hearted, treating everyone and everything with respect and courtesy. Compassionate and innately connected to the natural world around her, she even talks to the household pets, and forest creatures help dress her in the morning!

But perhaps it's Cinderella's selfless attitude toward her stepfamily that makes her a true Water-style character. While her stepmother and stepsisters fester with jealousy and greed, Cinderella stands apart as a truly empathetic caregiver. She exhibits the deep, thoughtful kindness characteristic of Water. As stories go, Cinderella teaches that a loving heart pays off in the end. I'm sure Prince Charming would agree.

Lieutenant Columbo

Water-style people exhibit strong intuition. Detectives in general fall under this category, but Lieutenant Columbo provides a very specific picture of Watery sensitivity. Played by Peter Falk on TV, Columbo is an unpretentious investigator whose affable demeanor throws suspects off guard. His contemplative manner illustrates Water's style of checking and rechecking facts against an internal lie detector. Someone's story either feels right or it doesn't.

Columbo is perceptive. He's a keen observer and sensitive to nuance, giving him the power to distinguish truth from fiction. When Columbo says his trademark "Oh, and one more thing," he's about to gain more evidence to prove what he already knows. Water style can see beyond words and sense another person's honesty or dishonesty.

Dorothy

Our heroine from *The Wizard of Oz* is a revealing example of Water style. The story begins when Dorothy gets caught in a tornado while rescuing her dog from a ruthless neighbor. She is willing to protect what she loves, even in the face of danger. Throughout her journey, Dorothy continues to show compassion by helping others less fortunate and taking them with her to Oz.

Dorothy's dream of returning home drives the story. She nurtures others but also wants to be nurtured. Water style loves the safety and protection of familiar surroundings. Could there a better symbol than home for safety and protection? I doubt it. "There's no place like home; there's no place like home" is a Water-style mantra for us all.

The Water You Are

Good Morning, Water

When the alarm goes off, you hit the snooze button and roll over. Why not? You're at home in dreamland and want to stay there as long as you can. Besides, it's just so comfy, safe, and snuggly under the covers that you don't want to break the spell right away and face the day. So maybe you hit the snooze button a few more times, sigh, and ease your body out of bed.

After finally getting up, you move to the window. The weather affects your mood, and you want to find out what kind of day you can expect. If it's raining or snowing, you might go back to bed and pull the covers over your head, at least for a while.

Eventually, your day gets going, and whenever possible, you take things at a nice, relaxed pace. Why rush when there's so much to enjoy about the morning routine? On goes the soothing music, and then it's off to the kitchen for a leisurely breakfast, preferably something warm and comforting such as oatmeal or buttered toast. The food not only nourishes your body, but it also stimulates your senses and feeds your artistic soul. A glass of orange juice causes an emotional reaction as you marvel at its vivid color and invigorating aroma.

After clearing away the dishes, you sit back and relax, sipping your coffee or tea while reading fiction or something inspirational. You may even take time to meditate or pray; it's important for you to feel centered and balanced before embarking on a busy day.

Now it's time for a long, hot shower. Aaahhh! That feels soooo good! The water flowing over your body makes you feel renewed, and you relish every drop. Standing there, you seem to go into a trance as your mind wanders from this to that. That's fine with you, because the shower is a great place for you to be in touch with your feelings and to let go of what's unresolved.

Getting dressed, you pick an outfit that suits your mood. If you're down, you might choose a colorful outfit to lift your spirits, or you may opt for something dark to complement how you feel. When you're feeling upbeat, you'll surely don cheerful colors and soft textures. Whatever you wear, it's an expression of your emotions and what's inside you.

As you walk out the door, you feel composed, together, and ready for the day. With plenty of time to get to your destination, you can even stop and smell the roses.

When We First Meet Water

Warm and sincere, you greet people with a heartfelt handshake or an enveloping hug. When you meet someone, you try to connect on an emotional level. It's all about treating people the way you like to be treated. You go out of your way to make someone feel accepted and welcomed, and leave no doubt that you're oh-so glad about the encounter.

Right away, others perceive that you're willing to listen and open up accordingly. People sense that you understand them in a profound way, and some have the impression you've met before. Drawn in by Water intensity and emotional depth, people move closer to you. They feel certain that you can intuit what is left unspoken.

On certain occasions, you will wait for people to approach. Let's say you're at an event that's crowded with new people to meet. You might stand by yourself for a while and see who comes over. This gives you the space to feel safe. Because you're easily affected by other people's emotional states, you don't feel compelled to meet and greet everybody.

More often than not, you trust your first impressions, and you should. They are usually dead-on. This may make you seem subdued or cautious when meeting certain people, but really it's just you feeling them out. In your heart, you know whether or not it feels right to see someone again.

Talk to Me, Water

For Water, talking is not just about the words; it's also about tone of voice, facial expressions, body language, eye contact, and the overall vibe. So while someone could tell you, "I'll try to make it to your opening," the person's nervous smile might leave you with the opposite impression.

Because your intuition always runs full tilt, you often know what others plan to say before they open their mouths. Sometimes people look stunned at how easily you can finish their sentences.

Still, you'd rather listen than speak, and you know how to project your feelings without words. Why use language to communicate when you have an entire pool of nonverbal cues? With a subtle smile, a mischievous wink, an icy glare, or an encouraging nod, you say volumes and clearly communicate your true feelings.

When you do speak, though, your words spring from the heart. Even when you are feeling shy, you will honestly put your feelings out there. *I love you. I understand. I care. You mean the world to me. I couldn't live without you. You make me so happy*. These expressions and more show your capacity to discuss your feelings.

No matter what you say, your sincerity comes to the surface. If you ask, "How are you?" you really want to know. It's you who remembers to ask about a friend's sick mother or someone's problem at work. Quick to listen to what's going on for others, you are slower to open up about yourself. But once a person has earned your trust, you'll definitely share your story and your feelings.

Playing with Water

Since Water is imaginative and artistic, you enjoy leisure activities from an inspired perspective. A day at the beach isn't just fun and sun; it's also about the poetry of the occasion, the serenity of the ocean, the brilliance of the light, and the profundity of the sky. This poetic, dreamy quality helps you retain your childlike fantasy and wonder. You're the one who can still build a kick-ass sand castle, complete with moat to defend against the rising tide.

Usually, you choose activities to match your mood. Visits to art galleries and museums let you indulge your love of color and expression. Movies allow you to release emotions as you empathize with the characters. When you want to unwind, nothing beats a nice, long hike in the great outdoors. The natural world is your cathedral, and you never get enough. Nature feeds your soul.

At games of skill and strategy, such as poker and chess, you have a decided advantage because you can read your opponents so well. While other people's quirks and expressions are dead giveaways, you remain indecipherable, raking in the chips. Even though you're a pro at expressing feelings, sometimes you're an ace at hiding them.

You love imaginative play, especially when it lets you express yourself emotionally. Acting in amateur productions or playing the cello in your living room gives you a chance to emote, emote, and emote some more. Fantasy games allow you to indulge your love of make-believe as well as exercise your skill at strategy and intrigue. How about just chilling out on a blanket and pondering shapes in the clouds? Sounds good to me!

Water Helps Out

You need to be needed and come alive when people depend on you. Always willing to play the rescuer or listen to somebody's problems, you live to improve the lives of those around you. You want to protect all living things and are a safe harbor for many. As a listener, you empathize and give others a feeling of security. When you help someone calm down and feel better, you feel better. Sometimes this can feel like a lot of responsibility, but you wouldn't have it any other way.

People view you as their sympathetic, imaginative, artistic friend. Beyond having a shoulder to cry on, they also get someone with an eye for decorating. You're an expert at creating harmonious environments, and you have a gift for picking colors, patterns, and fabrics that produce a desired mood. Thanks to your natural artistic sense, you just know what looks good and feels right.

People also rely on you for your intuition and sixth sense about others. When a friend wants to pick an office manager for her small business, she'll ask you to sit in on interviews with prospective employees. Later, your friend will ask, "What did you think?" When you tell her which person to hire, she doesn't hesitate to take your advice. It brings me back to the idea that Water is a good listener. Not only are you listening to others but you're also listening to yourself. Those inner hunches and that gut feeling are indispensable life jackets whenever you're called to the rescue.

Teaming Up with Water

Teaming up with Water is like having a private psychotherapist on board. You're the sensitive one, highly attuned to how everybody feels. Ready to assume the role of peacemaker when trouble arises, you appeal to people's better nature and keep the proceedings on an even keel.

You try to avert or resolve disagreements because you want to protect people and make sure they're treated with kindness. Seeing any type of injustice hurts you, and as a result you will serve as a moral compass in a group.

Open and accepting, you are a sounding board, receptive to all ideas; but your true gift is for returning the idea in a more appealing form. I know a team of people that just created a new restaurant. The Water person took the concept and ran with it. She developed the desired mood and environment, selecting everything from the lighting and décor to the music and uniforms. When the restaurant opened for business, people said the place just felt right. She had created a whole experience.

Art, art, and more art—that's your forte. Any team you join is guaranteed a visionary member. People find inspiration in the way you add depth to ideas, and Water knows how to plug into what makes the audience tick. Whether you're on an advertising team or hanging art at a friend's house, you pull all the pieces together and create beautiful results.

Getting in Deep with Water

When water makes love, emotional ecstasy is on tap. In sex, you go beyond the physical experience, however intense, and enter a realm of pure emotion. For you, lovemaking is so emotional that you dissolve into union with your partner. Feelings are complicated for Water, and the emotional life is complex, especially when it comes to sex.

Highly attuned to your lover, you are a natural expert at what feels good. Ultra-romantic, you want the lights dim, the sheets soft, and music that enhances the mood. You love anything that heightens physical sensations, including aromatic oils, hot baths, oysters, and champagne. Floating along on a sea of sensations, you are free to fully experience the moment.

That moment should feel safe, and when it does, you are truly uninhibited. You might laugh or cry for joy; either way, you are deeply moved. Lovemaking becomes mystical, enveloping, and intense. You come out of your body and merge with your partner in a great mingling of soul and flesh.

Water in the World

As far as work goes, you're most comfortable behind the scenes. This doesn't mean you can't be an actor or lawyer; you can. But for you, a fulfilling career is one that allows you to apply your overflowing sensitivity. Water people show up in professions where their compassion and insight can create change. You could be a photojournalist, shooting heartrending photos of refugees, a doctor in the refugee camp, or someone who works for a relief organization.

You're drawn to professions where your concern can make an impact. As a doctor, nurse, therapist, or other caregiver, you not only ease a patient's physical difficulties but also take time to listen and reassure.

A career in the arts represents another way you can express your sensitivity. Whether you choose acting, writing, design, painting, music, or dance, the arts offer you a safe place to express your emotions and explore your imagination. There is also an opportunity to bring the healing power of art to others.

Good fits for Water include professions where your gentleness and empathy can make a difference. Occupations such as estate and will planning rely on professionals with the sensitivity to serve the bereaved or the elderly. Counseling of any kind, from trauma work to working with high school kids, is also a good match for Water.

Water as a Friend

If a storm were brewing in my personal life, I'd call my Water friend. I know I could count on you to offer emotional support, listen, and care. You feel for people, and that makes you indispensable during emotionally charged times. And, really, when is life not emotionally charged? In good times and bad, we want our friends to show up for us. Water, that's you! You're not only present; you're involved.

Friends can always count on you for a hug! You offer warmth and closeness, and your affection and acceptance make words unnecessary. Depending on the circumstances, you may relate with joy and happiness or sadness and consolation. You serve as a source of comfort and understanding. (Dare I say warm and fuzzy?) Thoughtful and considerate, you remember birthdays and holidays, and you are the first to send a get-well card or remember someone's anniversary.

You're motivated by a desire to protect your friends. Upset when anyone feels uncared for or forgotten, you extend yourself to make sure people are safe and acknowledged.

Should someone need a professional referral, you are always good for a recommendation, whether it's a dentist, lawyer, or hair repair guru. People trust your suggestions because they know you would only direct them to the most caring, sympathetic, sensitive individuals.

At Home with Water

"Comfy-cozy" style originated with you in mind. Water needs to feel safe at home, so your surroundings are warm, enveloping, and quiet. Just give you a cushiony sofa, overstuffed chairs, and lots of throw pillows, and you're in paradise. A serene environment—that's the way you want to live, and your space reflects that in every corner.

With a lived-in look, but definitely not a mess, the Water home is a feel-good place. Cooking oils stand on the kitchen counter in whimsical dispensers, and the TV remote stays within easy reach. You are at ease and reassured in this relaxed environment, and don't need everything tidy and put away to feel comfortable.

Nostalgic and sentimental, you remain connected to the past, and memories are important to you. Perhaps your father purchased that whimsical oil dispenser during a family trip to Portugal, or maybe you bought it with your mom on a wonderful afternoon visit to the mall. Either way, the item reminds you of happy times and links you to your emotional life.

Your home engages all your senses. You may have an aquarium in the family room or a first-class entertainment system that keeps you relaxed and amused. So put up your feet and enjoy that favorite TV show or just close your eyes and listen to the music. At home, you can relax and leave those worries behind.

Be Water's Guest

What if everyone who got invited to your home made you feel good down to your soul? That's a Water party. Affectionate and caring, you know how to bring on the dreamy love vibes. So hug your guests, and then hug them some more. Your party is an emotional free-for-all, an extravaganza of good vibrations.

In your world, art and music are the focus of any get-together, and they create an emotionally groovy time. You're in tune with musical styles and love to share your latest finds with others. Since art speaks to you emotionally, you enjoy sharing your feelings about artistic creations.

Mystery and imagination inspire you, so a palm reader or psychic might work well at your party. Helping people to get in touch with themselves allows you to share what life is like for you. The Water world of emotions flows at your place, and art springs forth.

Water's Deeper Needs

Water, you are the emotional one. You're intuitive, imaginative, artistic, and sensitive. What you want most in the world is for other people to accept and validate your feelings.

The Deeper Needs of Water

- Having emotional validation
- Being reassured and understood
- Feeling nurtured and protected

With Water, nothing soothes like compassion. You need to feel understood and honored on an emotional level. You want people to appreciate your feelings, let you know everything will be okay, and always be there for you.

Water Outside and Water Inside

Water is a symbol for your elemental qualities. The chart below shows and compares how the attributes of water in nature correspond with these elemental qualities of Water in your personality.

WATER IN NATURE ELEMENTAL ATTRIBUTES	YOUR WATERY NATURE ELEMENTAL QUALITIES
Flowing	Imaginative, artistic, sensitive, emotional, considerate
Buoyant	Romantic, affectionate, loving, charismatic
Soothing	Supportive, helpful, caring, protective, peaceful, dedicated, domestic, nostalgic, tender, nurturing, self-sacrificing
Cleansing	Penetrating, responsive, sincere
Deep	Sympathetic, sensitive, intuitive, emotive, compassionate, empathetic, receptive, contemplative, introverted, intense
Reflective	Poetic, dreamy, meditative, inspirational, idealistic, musical, psychic, mystical

6
Earth Style: Practical

Mix one part efficiency and two parts precision,
fold them together with just the right amount of
no-nonsense usefulness, add a dash of good taste,
and you've got the recipe for Earth.

How in the world do we actually make things happen? With Earth energy, that's how! The ability to accomplish something in the tangible world is the Earth energy within you. Earth-style people live in that material reality. Their whole way of being is focused on practicality, organization, and substance. The power to manifest makes Earth people reliable and responsible.

The four fictional characters that follow represent the energy of Earth. They were chosen to show the variety in Earth's style. Because they are characters from our cultural mainstream, I like to think of them as the Earth we know.

Dr. Cliff Huxtable

Played by Bill Cosby in *The Cosby Show*, Dr. Huxtable is a dedicated family man. He is the kind of character who's easy to love. Despite a demanding job as an obstetrician, he manages to maintain his cool as the family patriarch. A hardworking and devoted nature is pretty fundamental for Earth style, and Dr. Huxtable shows up every time. His steadiness makes people feel at ease around him, and erratic is not even in his vocabulary.

Dr. Huxtable's respectable career is one of the reasons for his good social standing. Earth people are very concerned about the way they are perceived in the world, and a reliable reputation is important. For Dr. Huxtable, it means others can count on him. Loyal and trustworthy, he is the kind of good egg who will not only make you breakfast but also clean up afterward.

Carol Brady

The Brady Bunch made me laugh for much of my childhood, and I have a special fondness for Florence Henderson's character, Carol. Organized and totally on top of things, she could put on a play, plan a PTA event, get dinner on the table, and make it all look so easy. How could she not be organized? She ends up with six kids. Think about it: six kids. My goodness, that's a lot of juggling.

Yet through all her domestic duties and desire to be a modern woman, Carol Brady always had time to offer wise and reliable counsel. Hardly an episode went by where Mrs. Brady didn't turn out to be the prudent and thoughtful troubleshooter, offering sober advice and a practical solution. Earth-style practicality was something that just made sense for her.

Mary Richards

She could turn the world on with her smile, but I'll tell you what: she was the voice of reason in *The Mary Tyler Moore Show*. Played by Moore as TV's first successful, independent career woman, Mary

Richards was a breakthrough character who got ahead because she pursued her goals and ambitions diligently. There was no slacking in Mary's world.

Practical and down-to-earth, Mary was loyal and professional both in and out of the office. It's not as if she didn't have opinions or the space to express them; it's more that she was metered and thought things through before making them public. This stemmed from her Earth-style qualities of discretion and common sense, two virtues that allowed Mary to maintain her dignity in the face of some very odd friends and co-workers.

Santa Claus

Santa is the perfect picture of an Earth father. He's responsible, dependable, and kind. These enduring images of our favorite holiday fellow are as brimful with his stable character as his sleigh is with gifts. Hardworking and steady, Santa is productive. In fact, probably no other character in history produces the kind of gross domestic product that Santa comes up with.

Perhaps this is all because of his determination and tenacity. One can only imagine how much he has to focus on the goal in order to achieve it. Earth style is persistent that way, and Santa Claus doesn't seem to take no for an answer. He'll even fly in very bad weather. Oh, and one more thing I can't forget: all that list making and double-checking—that's Earth for sure.

The Earth You Are

Good Morning, Earth

Well, the expression "sleep like a rock" comes to mind when I think of Earth in the morning. It's not that you can't get out of bed easily; you can. It's more the comfort of the covers, the warmth of the mattress, and the safety of the pillow that leaves you wanting more sleep time. Yet you are the master of a well-organized routine, and greeting the morning is no exception. With your alarm clock set for precisely the right moment, you will rarely hit the snooze button. It is more likely that your preset coffeemaker has your favorite brew ready by the time you hit the kitchen.

Bathroom time is luxury time for Earth. Linen closets—in fact, all closets—are in picture-perfect order. Your bath towels are plush and sensual, and you love how they feel against your skin. While everything is sensible, that doesn't mean it's cheap or that you've spared any expense on products that make you look good and feel good. But again, there goes time, that pesky taskmaster. Better move on to the next bit of business, or you'll be late; and, heaven knows, Earth does not hurry!

In a way, you are the epitome of well dressed. A careful and traditionally tailored look suits you just fine. You have no trouble finding what you need because everything is organized in a way that makes your life more efficient. Clothing, whether it's in the dresser or on a hanger, is neatly arranged. Perhaps you even like laying out the day's outfit the night before; you're all for anything that can simplify and streamline your morning. I know an Earth-style guy who says, "I don't make decisions too quickly, but when I make them, I stick to them. What I'm wearing is important to me. That's why I take my time to decide how I'm going to look. I can't rush into that."

Morning is a time for getting quite a few things done, and your well-organized way of meeting the day pays off from the start. There are to-do lists and schedules, deadlines, and end-of-the-month balancing acts that need to be considered. But you figured out all of it in advance. Always on top of things, your planner, PDA, and organizer are all set to beep and chime to remind you to be on time for that important appointment.

Since routine and careful planning make you feel secure, you are hardly "on the run." Breakfast and getting out the door are practical and organized. That high-fiber bran muffin is as necessary as your electric garage door opener or excellent new cologne.

When you leave for the day, you are prepared. There's plenty of time to get to your destination, and you've remembered to bring everything you'll need when you get there.

When We First Meet Earth

Extremely inviting, yet not at all in-your-face, Earth is slow to get to know. There is a warmth about you that puts people at ease. Your friendly smile is welcoming, and your attractive demeanor reassuring. Even so, you are cautious about overextending your interest in someone, and you are reluctant to make fast friends.

This does not mean you are aloof. In fact, you feel it is far more sincere to get to know someone first. Better that than to proclaim undying love or jump in too quickly and then pull out and create hurt feelings.

Still, on first meeting, you are reliably available and open to hearing someone else's point of view while offering a polite and respectful attitude in return. "Manners, after all," one Earth-style person has been known to say, "are what separate us from the animals."

Along with that comes punctuality and a whole host of rules you are willing to abide by. Earth is never late, and you feel others should be on time too. You respect other people's time, and you expect them to respect yours. This may make you seem old-fashioned, but you believe a more traditional approach to human interaction makes for peace and harmony, and you like that.

Because of this, people find you dependable, whether meeting you for the first time or the hundredth. We rarely encounter the unexpected when dealing with Earth. This makes you comforting, and that gives people the relaxed space to be themselves with you too.

Dr. Craig Martin

Talk to Me, Earth

First of all, Earth is a good listener. So you are not usually the one doing all the talking. It's more important for you to give a well-thought-out response than to think out loud. This rational approach to life makes you a levelheaded conversationalist, and people are often surprised by your observations. You're grounded, and that makes your responses useful to your listener. Someone could walk away from a talk with you and have a tangible suggestion or idea to put to use right away.

Preferring to get right to the point, there's no room in your speech for ornate language or excess words. You would rather be succinct than talk for the sake of hearing yourself. This makes you thorough and careful when you explain something. You wouldn't consider skipping over anything important or including what's unimportant.

Basically, it takes a good reason to get you to open your mouth. You don't like wasting words on chitchat and are fonder of talking about things that mean something to you. From sports scores to a newfound recipe, you are more than willing to talk about the things that bring realness into your life.

And when it comes to opinion, you've got strong ones. Not that you are out there volunteering your view of the world, but when pressed, you will let someone know what you think. That's when your natural tact comes into play. You can present your ideas in a non-threatening way because people can see that you're not likely to speak without a great deal of forethought.

Playing with Earth

Really, you can have fun no matter what you're doing, as long as you have a few instructions and the right tools. In every undertaking, Earth is industrious, and play is no exception. Practical tasks are fun for you, so work is play in Earthland. Prepare Thanksgiving dinner? Varnish the back deck? Why, even sandblasting the house can be fun for you. That's because you have a different definition of the word "chore."

Getting things done gives you a lot of personal satisfaction. Being productive makes you feel good. You love how-to projects and are always ready to build on your practical skills and learn something useful. Just visiting the local hardware store or home remodeling center can be fun for you. Maybe you should pick up that new food processor. It looks time saving, like the leaf blower you bought during your last visit.

You see, for Earth there is real fun in making things, because then there's the fun of using them. Once you've finished making that new patio out back, it becomes all the more enjoyable to serve dinner there to someone special.

That brings me to the comfort-seeking Earth. Let's not forget that you are the ultimate lover of pampering. I don't know one Earth-style person who wouldn't be first in line for a good massage. When you're looking for fun, you need look no further than your favorite restaurant down the street or even your couch.

Earth Helps Out

You know, when I think of someone helping me out with my day, Earth style comes to mind. It's just in your nature to be helpful. No errand, chore, or task is beneath you. If someone needs you to pet-sit or hold a ladder, you are more than happy to oblige. People can count on you, and being dependable means something to you.

While others may talk about what they're going to do, you're busy doing it. You are a hard worker, and you know how to get a job done. Earth really rocks when it comes to commitment to a task. This kind of work ethic results in a very fine reputation. People actually say,

"You're very helpful." It's the truth, and you're pleased to be known as a giver.

Your talents are not just limited to being handy. You also have a head for practical solutions, and you're an expert at organizing and coordinating. Because of you, the job gets done, and efficiently too!

When you say, "Now, just wait a minute while I figure this out," it would be wise to give you that time. Many a dead end could have been avoided if people had listened to Earth's sound reasoning before starting a task. We could all use a little of that kind of help. "Haste makes waste" is surely one of your favorite expressions.

Once you've figured out the most efficient way to help, you don't need to talk too much about it. Staying focused is easy for you. If you've shown up to work, you work, and you don't get easily side-tracked. It reminds me of an Earth type I know whose relatives are always asking for help with family events. They just tell her the type of event, give her a few suggestions, and, like magic, she makes it happen. She's so good, but behind the scenes, it takes her countless hours of phone calls, skilled coordination, and proficient time management to pull it off!

Teaming Up with Earth

You are the anchor in any group. Not only are you reliable, but you also guide the direction and purpose of the team. You keep everyone focused on what's important. This is quite a challenge with so many opinions muddying things up. If there were a book fair to put on, you would see that books actually show up and that there's a place to display them and a cash box to collect the proceeds.

For you, it's all about results. Earth assumes the role of turning an idea into a tangible product, and no one does it better. You are determined, and obstacles are no match for your resolute drive. Fellow team members recognize your tenacity and respect your do-or-die approach. When you're on a team, people know to get out of your way. Once you get started on a path, you always cross the finish line.

Some might think of you as a steamroller. Perhaps this is true, but really you're dedicated to getting the job done. You are persistent. "If at first you don't succeed, try, try again" was first uttered by an Earth-style person. It's true!

So you are the solid part of the team, and you take your role seriously. If you're volunteering for a political candidate, you will go door to door to get out the vote; and if people need rides, you will drive them to the polling place. People can always count on you to do the heavy lifting and pull more than your weight.

Rock Solid with Earth

It's less about the music and more about the sheets for Earth. Sensuality is your middle name, and sex engages all your senses. From the feel of the bed linens to the smell of your partner's neckline, you are in mega-sensory bliss when making love. You like nothing more than to lie back and have someone else take charge. Your body loves to be held, stroked, and kissed, and there is no substitute for good old-fashioned touch. It's like your whole body is an erogenous zone, sensitive to both the pleasure of a gentle caress or a firm squeeze.

But let's not go too fast here; you want to take it slow. You don't like to be rushed, so this is no time to start. Earth can linger, and why not make a good thing last? You are definitely up for that. So slow it down and let your lover stroke your cheek or blow in your ear; that's the way to rock your world.

The take-your-time attitude about sex makes you a connoisseur of snuggling. Hugging and holding are just as important to you as any of the more intimate sexual activities. Your lover is in for a treat with your head-to-toe wraparound snuggle love. In fact, you are so good at this kind of lovemaking that you and your partner can enjoy an amazing sleep in the joy of each other's arms.

For a closer peek at the sex life of Earth style, all you need to know is that Earth is not afraid of sweat, body odor, human bodily function, or guttural noise. That said, it doesn't take a big imagination to figure out that when the Earth moves under your feet, you are in for a treat!

Earth in the World

People usually judge each other based on what a person does for a living, and Earth is acutely aware of that. For you, worldly standing is a statement of your worth as an individual. Since respect from others is integral to your self-image, it's critical that you feel good about your career. You spend years establishing a reputation as an upstanding and honorable member of society. You are diligent and committed to both your work and social standing. Earth-style people in my practice often ask, "How are people seeing me?" or "How did that make me look? Did that make me look bad?" For Earth, there is a strong desire for high esteem, and Earth-style work choices reflect that.

For that reason, Earth is the person who works long days, long hours, and lots of them. You are regimented, plan all your tasks and appointments well in advance, and definitely keep a full schedule. When people view you as hardworking and committed, you gain their respect.

Stability is the key here. Your practical nature makes you work hard; and, in the end, you earn a good reputation from it. Earth takes a less risky approach to career. "Slow and steady wins the race," you'll always say; and most of the time, you come out a winner.

While you might make the perfect accountant, there is far more to Earth than crunching numbers and folding towels. You excel in all professions that offer people tangible results. Architecture, dentistry, and banking are a few good places to find you.

Forestry, nature in general, and all kinds of detailed repair work are also a great fit. Perhaps carpentry, skilled labor, or even management and troubleshooting computer systems are where you're at. I know one thing: whatever you're doing, you are competent, and everyone thinks your work is great!

Earth as a Friend

I might want to spend Super Bowl Sunday at your house. You've got the awesome stereo and the best TV! Besides, you're going to have all the right snacks and beverages. As a friend, you are amazing in the most basic ways. Not only are you handy and helpful, but you're also ultracompetent. You're comfortable buying the food, cooking the meal, and cleaning up afterwards; and you make it all look so easy.

Your friends know how dependable you are. You're the responsible one, the designated driver if need be, the person everyone can rely on. You are definitely not a flake. In fact, you are loyal and willing to extend yourself to the max for your friends. In tough times, you are the rock, the fortress, the safe haven, and the place where friends can feel secure. People are lucky to have you as a friend, and you value the longstanding friendships that loyalty brings.

Developed over time, friendship for you is well thought out. You are not hurried and likely to go slowly when getting to know someone. For Earth style, friendship is something you invest in, and the dividends pay off over time. Not keen on surprises, and slow to anger, you like to know what to expect. So pass the chips; I think the game is starting.

At Home with Earth

In organized surroundings like yours, it's easy to unwind. Comfortable living is all around you. It doesn't matter if it's shabby chic or classic décor; your space is inviting. Clutter or disarray will only upset Earth's tranquil environment. A messy home, after all, is an agitated home. So a neat, clean, and orderly place is an Earth must!

Beautiful surroundings are next atop your list. All your furnishings, down to the kitchen appliances, reveal your fine aesthetic sense. The sofa is fluffed just right, and your wall art shows good taste in both content and form. Beyond the beautiful, your home is durable and reliable both inside and out. If you can't depend on something, you really don't need it around.

It's not as if you're completely traditional or conservative, although Earth is known for a conventional attitude toward living arrangements. It's more as if you want your home to work well and, at the same time, provide comfort and security for your deserving bones. Your home needs to make you feel good down to the details. I know an Earth guy whose household cleansers under the kitchen sink not only have all the labels facing forward, they smell good too!

So here at home you are content, comfy, and relaxed in your peaceful surroundings, an atmosphere of order that grounds you from the hectic world outside. It's a fine thing, this Earth home, where there is warm apple pie and plenty of throw pillows to go around.

Be Earth's Guest

You tend to be a pretty laid-back host, but if someone is twenty minutes late for your dinner party, that's not okay with you. The appetizer will have been served already but, hey, that's their problem. Punctuality aside, you are generous when it comes to party time. No detail is left unnoticed and no matter too small when party planning is in order. From the food to the decorating, everything is perfect. The music, the guest list—it's all top notch, and everything is coordinated and just right.

Not that all your events are formal, but even the most casual get-together should have a certain good taste as far as you're concerned. Turns out, your guests are always in for a first-class gathering.

I was invited to an event thrown by a terrific Earth-style gal. It was a re-creation of the last dinner on the *Titanic*. The hostess served the same menu from that fateful night, and all the guests were encouraged to come in formal voyaging attire. She observed many details from the actual time period. Even the wines were the same. The party was a delight, and I know she worked hard to pull off such a meticulously planned bash.

All the fussing over the details is not about impressing people. You just want everyone to enjoy themselves. The music is never too loud, and no one ever leaves hungry! Whatever it takes, Earth really knows how to make their guests feel comfortable.

Earth's Deeper Needs

Earth, you are the builder and the practical one. What you want most in the world is stability and reliability. You need to know that other people are dependable. Your well-being and comfort depend on having structure and security in your life.

With Earth, nothing comforts like steadiness. You want people to keep their word, show up on time, and value a basic code of loyalty and faithfulness.

The Deeper Needs of Earth

- Stability and responsible behavior
- Dependability and security
- Structure and comfortable surroundings

Earth Outside and Earth Inside

Earth is a symbol for your elemental qualities. The chart below shows and compares how the attributes of earth in nature correspond with these elemental qualities of Earth in your personality.

EARTH IN NATURE ELEMENTAL ATTRIBUTES	YOUR EARTHY NATURE ELEMENTAL QUALITIES
Fertile	Productive, industrious, hardworking, organized, steady, dutiful, systematic
Solid	Responsible, reliable, dependable, secure, stable, self-reliant, diligent, confident
Grounded	Practical, realistic, economical, sensible, pragmatic, domestic
Constant	Prudent, respectful, loyal, enduring, traditional, cautious, conservative, conforming, perseverant
Anchored	Serious, scholarly, upright
Firm	Fastidious, careful, slow to anger, contemplative, persistent, tenacious

Part II

Intimacy and Working It Out

7

Intimacy and the Road Trip of Love

*N*ow that you know something about your elemental style, let's look at how to make the most of it, starting with intimacy!

The Foundation of Intimacy

Most adults want to be in a close relationship. The main reasons are to love another and enjoy that person's company. But I think there's more to it. Something else drives us to want relationships. I think of it as a deeper, universal need. That need is intimacy. Your desire for a relationship is part of a collective search to meet this universal need. It is a search we are all in to find true intimacy.

The kind of true intimacy I'm referring to is not hand-holding or sexual intimacy. I'm talking about getting to know someone and having that person get to know you—and I mean more than knowing your name and what you do for a living. Getting to know each other means finding out how you affect each other. Intimacy is about openness with truth.

Entering into a romantic relationship is like agreeing to go with another person on a road trip. You hope it's a long and enjoyable journey, and you want it to be fun. There will be pictures and memories and laughter and little surprise pecks on the cheek. There is so much to share—your likes and dislikes and all the things in life that make you smile or look on with wonder. But at the same time, close proximity for an extended period means sharing everything, and that brings certain issues to the surface.

It can be hard enough to just get across town in the same car with some people. What do you do with someone who talks too much? What about someone who doesn't like your music? Or constantly tells you how to drive? Or, worse yet, has bad manners?

Getting to Know You

Walking down a country road at night to look at the stars is wonderful. It's even better with a special someone who likes looking at stars too. Sharing common interests with someone you like is amazing. And even if you come to find out that he or she gets cold faster than you and wants to go back inside, you don't have to get disappointed or angry. Next time you could choose to accommodate your companion's need, bundle them up a bit better, and stay out longer.

When your relationship with someone is more casual, well, the trip is short, and you just hang on until they get out of the car. But a romantic relationship is different. This relationship is intended to last a lot longer. So you're going to have to deal with those issues that pop up from being together so much. That's a big part of intimacy, and it is not always easy.

Getting to know someone can be difficult because of the disappointment, anger, or hurt that you may encounter. Even though you may feel like getting out of the car, perhaps this is one trip you would really like more of. Well, that's going to mean dealing with those difficult feelings. Your traveling companion goes through the same thing with you. You see, needing to be known and accepted is complicated, but it is the deepest motive for wanting a connection in the first place. Intimacy is not only the reason for the road trip, but because it creates a real connection, intimacy is also what makes your time spent together truly worthwhile.

Intimacy = Realness

If you travel in the car with someone for days or weeks on end, your companion will probably get to know the whole you. Mostly, that's a good thing. You make each other laugh, you enjoy experiences together, and you create a foundation of love that you can look back on. But the real you is more than just a perfect picture. The real, complete you, and all you are capable of, is bound to show up over time, and that can be pretty frightening—for both of you! Intimacy is difficult because it's not always easy to face or reveal the complete you.

Scary questions can arise. What's going to happen when you're not happy or your partner isn't happy with the entire you? What happens if your partner thinks you talk too much? What happens if you're distractible and you get lost? Will you get blamed? Will you get criticized? You could become really defensive. How will you handle all that? These questions create fear, and they make entering into an intimate relationship more difficult. But fear not, for all is not lost!

The better you know who you are, the better you can handle intimacy. When you know yourself, your traveling companion has a much easier time of it too. If you're aware of your needs and know the best ways of expressing them, then things have a better chance of working out.

> *The better you know your complete self,*
> *the easier you'll find the process of intimacy.*

Revealing Your Complete Self

Intimacy doesn't happen all at once. Some road trips are longer than others. The road trip of a lifetime is usually preceded by a few shorter ones. So recognize that intimacy can come in doses and in varying levels. You could think of it as "Getting to know someone takes time." Still, intimacy involves revealing yourself to someone else, whether it happens quickly or over a period of time.

Your relationship often creates a new awareness about yourself. Beliefs you developed about yourself in your early years may remain unquestioned; then a relationship comes along and—wham!—those beliefs get challenged.

"I don't get why she just called me unaffectionate! I'm affectionate. I just don't like holding hands in public. Hmmm, does that mean I'm not affectionate? Now what?"

"Why does my partner say I'm a complainer, when really it's that I'm just emotionally expressive? Who's right here?"

"I can't say, 'I love you'; that's weak and dangerous. But other people do it. What do I do?"

"I think everything is going great! I'm awesome, so why is it that he doesn't want to move it along faster? There must be something wrong with him. It couldn't be me, could it?

There are many variations on what you believe about yourself, along with many questions about how you need to act. In relationships, many of those beliefs surface in your own mind first, often as your fears. Sometimes your partner might point out these beliefs, attitudes, or fears to you. Sometimes you may just act them out. Either way, revealing yourself to someone else can be frightening. What will happen if you reveal some aspect of yourself and it's a deal breaker? That can be the scariest part.

Hiding Your Complete Self

Some relationships look as if two people get along, but really it's an illusion created by one or both partners shutting down. Someone hides his or her feelings or real self to the point where there is no intimacy. This happens when one partner is afraid of the other or when someone is afraid to look within. Basically, the individual hides his or her feelings to make the relationship work out. But this is not an honest relationship. It is a self-deception, created by either an internal fear of the self or an external fear of the partner.

What if you get in the car and your partner wants the music really loud, but you want to talk? Can you say so? Do you need to? Will you feel too afraid to let your needs be known? I hope not! When you're intimate with your partner, it means that somehow you will say what's on your mind and voice what you need. But how?

Love makes it possible to share yourself with someone.

Love, Honesty, and Inner Growth

The road trip of intimacy can be a lot easier if you bring along your road kit. Breakdowns can occur, and it's good to have tools along. In your relationship, the kit includes love, honesty, and inner growth. Intimacy is incomplete without all three.

Love

Love is perhaps the most ethereal and hard to define of these three. It's part desire and part caring. Desire is more like the passion part of love, and caring is more like the nurturing, protective, and "concerned for someone's welfare" part. When combined, the desire and the caring add up to a feeling that makes us want to be with someone. You wouldn't take this trip if you didn't want to be with the other person. The enjoyment in spending time together is the starting point.

Love, you already know, is a huge part of your relationship. Love makes it possible to share yourself with someone. It keeps you at the table. When the going gets tough, love works its magic and you stay connected. When you love the other person on the road trip, you're more likely to care when things go wrong. But love itself does not a relationship make.

Honesty

Honesty is also essential. Without it, you can't have a meaningful relationship. It is difficult to imagine how any relationship can survive without honesty. That's why honesty needs to be in the road kit.

Sadly, dishonesty is a key reason why relationships don't work out. I can't begin to count the number of times that one deception or another has led to a lack of trust in a relationship. Often, distrust is the end of a relationship altogether. I'm not referring only to infidelity. There are many ways to be dishonest.

Maybe when I agreed to go on this journey, I didn't tell my partner that I can't drive after dark and that I need to stop every two hours for a bathroom break. Worse yet, I lied about it and let my partner find out in the middle of the ride. Yikes! That wasn't fair or honest!

Then there's another whole layer to honesty. Part of the honesty within intimacy is honesty with yourself. It's the self-honesty you have about your own actions, words, or personality. On the road trip, perhaps you've tried to control your partner's driving. By taking an honest look at yourself, you notice your behavior. Then you become conscious that you're a backseat driver. You've told your partner to drive with both hands on the wheel, where to make a turn, and how closely to follow the car in front of you. You ask yourself, "Is my partner really driving badly?" If not, you ask, "Why is it so hard for me to let go and give my partner some space?" This is where intimacy begins to get tough. Can you "own your stuff" and be honest about it? The love part—well, that comes naturally, but honesty is not always so easy.

Inner Growth

Inner growth is built on self-honesty. It is the third quality that's essential for intimacy. Relationships make you grow, and that's something you need to accept as part of the process. If you have a desire to grow and a realization that you're not already perfect and that you have room to be better, then that helps your relationship from the start.

Between love, honesty, and inner growth, it is inner growth that presents the greatest challenge. That's because we all struggle with change, and inner growth is about changing yourself.

People express a beautiful sentiment when they say, "My relationship brings out the best in me." This means that when you are with your intimate partner, you are growing in a positive way.

On the road trip, your partner is someone you want to share with, explore with, treat with politeness, act kindly toward, and treat well in general. When you're with your partner and being your best self, you like yourself. That's a really good thing to find out, and it comes from inner growth.

Whether it's a conscious or unconscious choice, inner growth is a major reason that people seek relationships. It is like this mysterious benefit. You enjoy this wonderful love experience, plus you get to learn about and live honestly with another person and grow for the better. What could be more fulfilling? No wonder you want a good relationship!

Intimacy is a process of honesty,
reinforced by love that causes inner growth.

Dynamic Inner Growth, You Dig?

Inner growth is what happens when you look at your personality and decide to make a change. It always happens in good relationships—not because your partner wants to change you but because you want to change yourself into a more loving person.

The word "dynamic" means change, so the inner growth that causes us to change is called dynamic inner growth, or DIG. Three qualities—love, honesty and inner growth—are necessary for intimacy, but DIG presents the greatest struggle. It's difficult because changing yourself is hard, even though it makes you a better person.

Dynamic inner growth (DIG)
is the self-chosen, personal change that
happens when you reflect on your own actions,
behaviors, and thoughts.

People always say that "relationships are work," and it is your personal inner growth that is that work. Anytime you do work on yourself, not only do you grow for the better but your partner and relationship benefit too.

On the car ride, you and your partner need to decide so many things. What's your driving speed? Who's going to drive, when, and for how long? What music will you listen to? Where will you stop along the way?

Negotiating all these choices can be fun, and mostly it's easy. When you and your partner are in agreement, the best parts of your personality show up. But when you don't agree, the less desirable parts of your personalities can emerge. That's when you might "act out." You might speak harshly, clam up, be insulting or judgmental, and then . . . inner growth is the only way to move forward!

You will have to dig into yourself
for DIG to happen.

Intimacy and Your Elemental Style

How you express intimacy and the way you accomplish DIG depends on your elemental style. In upcoming chapters, I will explore this idea in more detail. For now, let's just say that each element—Fire, Air, Water, and Earth—has to do a specific type of work to achieve intimacy with his or her partner. Before I move on to the specific intimacy styles of the elementals, let's look at the general process of intimacy that all styles participate in.

The Process of Intimacy

Intimacy involves a process. This process is composed of a number of choices that are grounded in love, honesty, and inner growth. They aren't easy, but your readiness to make these choices is the only way a real connection with someone is even possible.

Choosing to Take Responsibility

You can't expect your partner to be a mind reader. You have to take responsibility for sharing your needs. How else will your partner know what you need?

I often encounter individuals who feel it should be unnecessary to ask for what they need. Well, it's not. In fact, it's the only responsible way of learning whether your partner can meet your needs. Sure, sometimes your partner will meet your needs without prompting, but that's seldom when trouble occurs. When you take responsibility for your needs, you'll find out whether your partner can meet them.

During the road trip, you can prevent aggravation if you tell your partner something sooner rather than later. What if you don't like the music? Maybe your partner thinks the music is okay with you. If you don't take responsibility for voicing your needs, then you could be headed for a problem.

Every time you tell your partner what you need,
your relationship becomes more authentic!

Choosing to Share Your Needs

Intimacy means opening yourself up and expressing your needs in an honest way. With the foundation of a loving heart, an honest conscience, and a desire to grow, you are able to move forward.

It's important to share your needs with your partner. This isn't about nitpicking or picking your partner apart. Sharing your needs happens best when it matters. Prioritize when to share your needs with your partner so that it matters when you say something.

On the road trip, you may need a partner who acknowledges all your great choices—the route, the stops along the way, the pictures you've taken. Maybe you need a partner who is flexible about going off the main road and exploring out-of-the-way places. Maybe you need a partner who can take it slow, roll down the windows, and absorb the mood or all the details.

As you share your needs, you'll realize how important it is to open up with each other. Every time you tell your partner what you need, your relationship becomes more authentic. When you find someone who can meet your needs, you'll find that you're really happy.

Meeting Your Partner's Needs

It's amazing to find someone who meets your deeper needs. But if the relationship is going to work out, you will also have to meet your partner's needs. Knowing your partner's deeper needs can help you understand whether you can meet those needs.

Choosing to Confront with or without Confrontation

Voicing your needs can seem confrontational. Sometimes it may actually need to be. If you feel scared because the car is going too fast, you may need to say, "Slow down!" It may be the only way to get through to your partner and let him or her know what's going on for you.

But most of the time there is a way of confronting someone without having to be confrontational. If you've been listening to the same CD for the last three hundred miles, you may say, "If I listen to this one more time, I'll scream," or "I haven't picked the music since the trip started." But this is just voicing your frustration, not your needs. This is being confrontational.

Confronting someone with your needs does not always have to be confrontational. Why not ask, "Can I pick something to listen to now?" Or "I'd like to listen to something else now, please." It might make it a whole lot easier. Your partner might not get defensive, because you're expressing your needs without attacking them.

Even when you confront your partner in the most skillful manner, vulnerable feelings could get created. Vulnerable feelings are normal, and they are necessary in the process of intimacy.

Choosing to Be Vulnerable and Deal with Defensiveness

Sharing and confrontation can create feelings of vulnerability. Most of us don't like hearing the words "I need to tell you something." Generally, we all think, "Oh no, what now?" We immediately feel the nakedness of our personality, and it's not the safest feeling. We can also feel vulnerable when expressing our needs to someone else because he or she may not meet them.

During the road trip, perhaps you've just navigated through a foggy mountain pass and want your partner to acknowledge your skillful driving. Instead, your partner says nothing. You want to ask for a pat on the back but might feel vulnerable about doing so. What if your partner can't provide what you need? At the same time, if your partner realizes you're hurt, he or she might feel vulnerable for not saying you did a great job. "Am I somehow a bad partner?"

Vulnerability is complicated. It creates feelings of guilt, shame, inadequacy, imperfection, stupidity, unworthiness, and smallness. Blah! Who wants to feel this way? But we do, and when we do, we become defensive. Vulnerability and defensiveness often result in anger, and anger makes working it out so much harder.

Still, defensiveness is a natural reaction that stems from a desire to protect yourself and your needs. In every relationship, there is some degree of vulnerability and defensiveness. Since vulnerability makes you feel exposed, you react by becoming defensive. For your relationship to stay honest, it's essential that you recognize the link between vulnerability and defensiveness and how to manage them.

So if, after making it through that mountain pass, you need some praise but instead your partner jokingly says, "Yeah, thanks for not crashing the car," you could feel hurt. Then you get angry and say, "Well, if you were driving, we would have been killed."

This kind of reaction is normal even though there might be better ways of responding to hurt feelings. The good part of defensiveness is that it can be used to find out what we need. After the disagreement, you can explain what you really needed and why you felt hurt and got defensive. It helps your partner understand what to do the next time. Even vulnerable and defensive feelings are part of the intimacy process.

Choosing to Manage Your Anger

There are whole books on anger management, and I have no intention of tackling all its complexities here. I'd just like to point out that we can all justify our anger. When your partner makes you angry, you feel entitled to your anger. But the point of intimacy is to move beyond what the other person did, figure out how to be honest with each other, and move on. Anger serves some purpose in the moment. It protects you by telling your partner to back off. But holding on to unresolved anger or perpetuating anger with stubbornness will not bring your relationship to higher ground.

So when you're on the road trip and need to take a step back for a moment, that's okay. That's good. You can pull over. You can get out for a minute. Just keep in mind that you don't need to hold on to your anger. You can move on. So get back in the car!

Recognizing that a partner who loves you is not the enemy makes it easier to choose trust.

Choosing to Trust

Trust takes time to develop. You are probably aware of the pitfalls of trusting someone too soon. You end up getting hurt because you haven't given the relationship enough time to build trust.

Nevertheless, I always trust first rather than make people earn my trust. If someone is untrustworthy, he or she will reveal it soon enough. A traveling companion who agrees to pay for half the gas and then shows up with no money will only last for that first tank!

Recognizing that a partner who loves you is not the enemy makes it easier to choose trust. That's because trust is the belief that your feelings and needs matter to your partner. So even when you need to confront each other and it hurts, you will know that your partner is on your side. You can trust the other person to work things out in the interest of fairness, truth, and meeting one another's needs.

It would be unwise to get into the car with a person you don't trust. Your relationship needs trust in order to achieve intimacy. Without it, you can't possibly share yourself with someone. Only by choosing trust will you feel safe revealing who you are, being vulnerable, and sharing your needs.

When you get in the car with your trusted companion, you will already know that they care enough to meet your needs. Over time you won't even have to say, "Slow down." Your companion will already know the right speed.

Choosing Willingness and Commitment

Willingness is the desire to engage in intimacy, and commitment is the dedication to follow through and see where your relationship leads.

When you agree to go on the road trip, do so willingly and with your eyes open. How can it possibly work out if you're not present, willing, and able to do the work?

I knew a couple who kept dating for years because the woman wasn't convinced that the man was committed. He kept telling her he was ready, and he finally convinced her. She gave in and agreed to get married. After marrying him, moving in, and making major changes to her life, the reality of commitment sank in for him. Within three months, he wanted out. Intimacy and being real was more than he had bargained for.

He may have thought he was ready, but really he had deceived himself and her. His willingness and commitment turned out to be superficial, and he ended up causing a lot of pain. When you enter into a relationship, you have an effect on another person's life, so you have an obligation to choose willingness and commitment as a part of intimacy.

Choosing Awareness

The complete picture of your character comes into sharper focus in romantic relationships. Your partner acts as a mirror where you can see your strengths and imperfections in finer detail. A good relationship includes compliments on your good qualities as well as pointing out the parts you need to work on. But most of us don't have a problem with the compliments!

You may think you're a great driver and want to be at the wheel all the time, but you've been stopped twice for speeding in the last three hours. You keep saying, "It's the cop's fault," and then your partner tells you, "Actually, Danica, you're driving like you own the road!" It's a good thing that love, honesty, and inner growth are in your travel kit!

The difficulties with intimacy begin when you become more aware of yourself and the parts that need work. Sometimes you can be self-aware and recognize on your own when your behavior needs improvement. But, like most people, you may be unaware of many aspects of your personality. You may not know that certain traits or behaviors exist until someone points them out to you. Your choice to hear these things about yourself, even when it's not easy, is another step toward a true connection with your partner.

Awareness is hard. The image you've constructed about yourself may not be entirely complete. Still, you reinforce that image with a career, a relationship, and a whole lifestyle. The "who I am" in life speaks loud and clear to people around you, but your image is only a partially accurate picture of who you really are. People often believe this incomplete picture to avoid parts of themselves that need work, yet avoidance might be just the cause for a road-trip-halting flat tire!

Unconscious actions and behaviors stem from
personality traits you don't even recognize in yourself.
This lack of awareness makes it difficult to be
honest about your role in any problem.

You see, your self-image is likely to cause a roadblock on the trip. A conflict will arise between who you think you are and who the relationship is revealing you to be. Any part of your self-image that is inaccurate will get broken down for you, and you'll have to deal with it.

The bright side to all these relationship-generated revelations is that you have someone right there in the car with you who can help you fix the flat! Becoming aware through your partner's observations is not easy or always pleasant, but it's a big part of this journey. As partners, you are there for each other. And awareness? You can do it!

Choosing Courage

All this awareness takes courage. Oh, how the bravest of us cower in the face of honest intimate connections. You don't like to fight, so you back down. You don't want to see your dark side, so you overpower your partner with anger, guilt, or blame. You're afraid to rock the boat. Courage is the ingredient that outweighs fear and allows you to demand the truth of yourself and from your partner.

With courage, you stand in the elemental intensity of intimacy, even when it's scary, exhausting, or frustrating. When you're truly intimate, conversations can get intense, tempers can get heated, emotions can erupt, tears can flow, and you might even end up doing the dishes, getting flowers, or buying a card!

To work it out, you have to do whatever it takes. You will need courage to do these things. Maybe you feel like jumping out of the car at the next red light. Don't! Even though you're uncomfortable now with all this intimacy, stay and work on your issues. It can't get better if you quit.

Your readiness to make the choices that encourage intimacy is a sign that you are prepared to have a meaningful relationship. Making those good choices is not always easy, but doing it increases the chances that your relationship will work out.

The Good, the Bad, and the Ugly of Intimacy

Intimacy can hurt, and that makes it difficult. It can hurt if we touch someplace in ourselves that's not easy, familiar, or resolved. Perhaps you think you need to be perfect. Your traveling companion could point out that your feet smell or that you're way too sloppy. Maybe they even want to just get out of the car and go home. Sometimes we can be so afraid of the possible hurts of intimacy that we don't even try to attain it. For people who won't try, intimacy is next to impossible.

There are other traits that offer a slim chance of having a healthy relationship. Dishonesty, being judgmental, and an unwillingness to grow preclude intimacy. Even worse is someone's refusal to look at dishonesty, being judgmental, and an unwillingness to grow. Active addicts, pathological liars, and chronic takers fall into this category. Unless something changes, it can be hard to get close to these people.

Intimacy is also difficult with those who are profoundly defensive, extremely quick to anger, or so afraid of inner growth that they are irretrievably in denial about themselves. These folks don't want to look at themselves or change. It's not that people can't get close to them, but it's tough.

Intimacy Can Be Easier

When you use *Elemental Love Styles* as a guide to learning more about yourself, it's a move toward having an accurate picture of who you really are and what you really need. That makes finding a great relationship and staying in one easier. There's no need to trap or manipulate anyone. Intimacy is all that's needed.

Remember, honesty is essential for intimacy. The more honest you are about your feelings and behaviors, the more self-aware you become. The more self-aware you become, the more honest you can be with yourself. It's awesome!

Intimacy and Romance

Romance is great. We all want romance in our relationships and everyone likes it when his or her partner expresses that little extra something. Romance is an important part of intimacy. It represents those gestures that make you feel loved and cared for. On a road trip, you don't want every meal to be drive-thru. It's the special dining spots that will make the trip memorable.

Making romantic gestures tells your partner, "I'm thinking of you," or "I think you'll like this." Also, a simple gesture can make your partner feel special. The notion that romantic gestures need to cost money is just not true. Romantic behavior can be as simple as saying "I love you," and it usually delivers the message, "I know you."

Knowing your partner and being known by your partner is a huge part of intimate relationships, and romance is one way of expressing the knowing. When we cook someone their favorite meal on a day they get a raise at work, it shows them we care and that we know them. We recognize when something is meaningful to them.

Romance conveys to your partner that you took the time to think of them and what they like. If you know that your partner likes to hold hands, then when you reach out to hold hands first, you've made a romantic and intimate gesture. The right gesture comes from knowing what they like.

Of course there are many universal gestures of romance: dinner out, flowers, soft lighting, and sexy lingerie to name a few. But when your relationship develops with intimacy, you also learn which flowers your partner likes and in what colors. Romance makes intimacy more complete because it gives you an opportunity to express that you know someone in a fun way.

Some people confuse romance with love. The danger in relying too heavily on romance for relationship happiness is that love is not a series of romantic gestures. Romance is a way of showing the love, but it is not the love. Love involves acceptance, honesty, and commitment. Romance may be the gravy of relationships, but love and intimacy are the meal.

Taking Your Time

Mastering intimacy doesn't come easily. It definitely doesn't happen overnight. This is a road trip, after all, so take your time. What's the rush? Intimacy is something you get better at with practice. You can expect to experience many great things along the way, but realize that it won't always be easy.

When you're close to someone for a long time, it's never easy. So be patient with yourself and your partner. Honesty, inner growth, courage, and responsibility are a challenge. Make some space to learn and grow. When you have a commitment to enjoy the ride and hang in there for the hard parts, it gets easier.

Intimacy Skills

We could all use a driving lesson every now and then. Knowing the rules of the road helps us navigate and makes the trip work out better. Intimacy skills are a three-point method for working it out with your partner in a more productive way. Remember, take your time. Intimacy is something that takes a lifetime, so go easy.

Intimacy Skills

1. Be gentle. Rather than saying, "We've got to talk!" approach your partner with, "Can I ask you something?" "Can I mention something to you?" or "Would it be okay to bring something up right now?" Acting in a gentle manner helps prevent defensiveness.

2. Be considerate. Speak for yourself and about yourself. Say, "When you talk to me like that, I feel stupid or put down," or "When you act like that, I feel embarrassed." Don't say, "You're demanding," or "You're embarrassing me." If you can speak for yourself and tell your partner where you're coming from, you're less likely to make your partner become defensive. Consideration for the other person's place in the relationship means speaking for yourself. Not saying, "You make me feel ..." but saying, "I feel ..."

3. Be open-minded. Make sure you listen to your partner's responses. Are you hearing the other person correctly? It's better to ask, "What do you mean by that?" than to act, respond, or reply based on an incorrect assumption.

When most couples try to work it out, they lack the intimacy skills to make things better. Instead, they get defensive and make things worse. Defensiveness compounds a problem, making it snowball into a bigger problem. As a result, people become distant because they don't really know how to connect.

Intimacy is a great journey because you get to learn so much about yourself and your partner. It's not always easy, but I promise you, it's totally worth the effort. Loving someone makes you a better person. How cool is that!

8

Working It Out: Dynamic Inner Growth and the Laundry of Love

I've spent a lot of time focusing on intimacy. That's because intimacy makes your relationship meaningful and real. One of intimacy's major components is dynamic inner growth, or DIG. DIG is about making better choices. It enables your relationship to work out better. A lasting relationship is one where you are going to have to work it out. You can't run, blame, or become immobilized by fear. You will need to work it out! Here's how.

What Is DIG?

DIG is the inner change brought about by self-reflection. I call dynamic inner growth DIG because it takes work, but the results are astounding. DIG can help you achieve a successful relationship, get what you need, and grow into your best self. All it takes is a readiness to grow.

> *DIG is the inner changes that occur through introspection.*
> *You don't just work it out—you dig it out!*

DIG happens through introspection. Simply put, DIG occurs when you take a look at your stuff. You then have the opportunity to make better choices. This means choosing between the negative side and positive side of your personality.

Negativity is still a choice, even if an unconscious one. If you act in an aggressive, dismissive, manipulative, or rigid manner, you actually choose to behave that way. Maybe you're unaware that you're making a choice. If you were more conscious of your behavior, you'd realize that you could react in other ways.

DIG opens up an opportunity to choose with awareness. By looking at your own actions, you can decide how to act. You are not simply at the mercy of a bad set of personality traits. You have control. In the end, most people prefer to choose the positive over the negative. DIG is the way.

Laundry list: The negative characteristics in your personality that you need to take a closer look at

DIG work qualities: The part of you that needs a little cleaning up, or what you could work on to make your relationship better

I call the negative qualities you need to look at your laundry list. These qualities are individual to you, and the laundry list is your own. In the chapters that follow, I will discuss how each elemental type experiences DIG. For now, just understand that DIG is something you do to work it out with your partner.

DIG is very much like doing your dirty laundry. It's something we all have to do. We may not like to think about it too much. That's why we keep it in the closet. We certainly don't like other people to see it. That's why we throw it under the bed when unexpected company comes over. You might not like to do it at all. Sometimes it's just so gross. But if you don't do your dirty laundry, it creates a problem.

The same thing applies to your personality. Behaviors that stand in the way of a successful relationship are the ones that could use a little cleaning up. These behaviors are the dirty laundry of your character. When you are intimate for an extended period of time, the laundry becomes more difficult to hide.

But any effort that you put into looking at these qualities is a victory for you and your relationship. The dynamic inner growth that your relationship encourages brings you closer to your better self— you know, brighter whites and more vivid colors. Wow!

Baggage or Laundry?

Often we look at prospective partners and assess the baggage they bring into a relationship. At the same time, we are acutely aware of our own baggage. But baggage refers to the parts of your past that you carry with you into the present. It is not something you can change. An ex-spouse, children from a previous relationship, bankruptcy, or even an STD can be the baggage of a person's past. Baggage is part of your history, and you need to bring it along because it is part of your life.

On the other hand, your laundry list is something you can change. By becoming more aware of your behavior, you can choose to change the way you behave. That's what DIG work accomplishes. Your ex-partner may be the baggage in your life, but letting him or her continue to walk all over you is your laundry.

You may be able to incorporate your baggage into your life in a positive way. After all, children from a previous relationship are usually good baggage, and even an ex doesn't have to be bad. You can't erase your baggage from your past.

The laundry list of your personality is another thing. You can look at your negative traits. While you may bring your character flaws with you from your past, you don't have to dump them on your partner in the present.

No one is ever forced to grow.

DIG: The Necessity

Two people in a relationship inevitably have differences. Sometimes you can easily resolve those differences, and sometimes you can't. Every now and then you may even get into a fight. Obviously, it's not a physical fight; it is more like a heated exchange or disagreement where feelings get hurt. DIG begins when you look at your part in a disagreement.

DIG is something you choose to do. No one is ever forced to grow. You could simply choose not to own your part in the argument and make it all about your partner. One of the biggest reasons relationships fail is because people are reluctant to dig into themselves and grow. You may be happy just the way you are, but that doesn't mean your intimate partner likes the way you are all the time. And if you really think there's nothing wrong with you and the issues in your life are about everyone else, then you really need to start digging.

The laundry list of your personality is the entire set of characteristics that could use some work. If you are honest about yourself, you can see what needs improvement. Cleaning up that laundry makes you so much easier to get along with. After all, it's really hard to be with someone who doesn't do his or her laundry.

To do this work, you need to be willing. Remember, the payoff for looking inside yourself is a better, more honest relationship. So let's clean up this mess. Once you know your deeper needs and commit to working it out, DIG can be fun. Finding someone who wants to do the laundry with you is truly amazing!

The Beginning of DIG

When you and your partner have a disagreement and feelings get hurt, ask yourself these questions (any or all might apply):

1. Do I have a part in this?
2. What is my part in this?
3. Do I need to apologize?
4. Do I think my partner should apologize?
5. How did we get here?
6. Am I holding on to something (acting unforgiving)?
7. Can I forgive my partner?

DIG Occurs in Two Ways

DIG occurs in one of two ways, either by confrontation or observation. Both of these can cause you to self-reflect.

Confrontation is the most common way that people become aware of their laundry lists and DIG work qualities. Your partner tells you, in effect, "Your clothes are dirty." Then he or she spells it out for you, saying exactly what you did wrong or how you're behaving. If someone says, "You're ignoring me, so please stop," you might want to look at whether you've given the other person enough attention.

When it's done in a positive way, confrontation is called feedback or constructive criticism. Everyone gets comments like these from parents, siblings, bosses, and friends. Most of the time, if you're not too defensive, you sit with feedback, think about it, and make a change. When your partner says you're talking kind of loud in a fairly quiet coffee shop, you might think about it and lower your voice. No problem. That's DIG.

The second way DIG happens is through observation. Sometimes no one has to point out that the laundry needs attention. You just know. In relationships, this might happen when you see your partner cry or get upset during an argument. You reflect on your actions and figure out why and how you upset your partner without the other person saying anything. Let's say you're stressed and snap at your partner, biting the person's head off for no reason. You might catch that right away and quickly apologize. When you figure it out on your own, that's DIG too.

Through confrontation and observation, you get a better idea of what to work on in yourself. Remember, this inner work helps make your relationship better. No one is perfect. We all have laundry, so we all have something to work on. Let's find the right space to do that.

A DIG Story, Part 1: Confrontation

A couple has been together for a few years. Essentially, the two people are very happy with each other. Each year in the summer, they travel a few hundred miles to visit one of their families.

Every year, it seems as if the partner scheduled to visit the in-laws has some complaint. When the summer trip rolls around, typical behavior includes whining, distance, petulance, and pouting.

This year, though, the disgruntled partner gets confronted. "Why are you behaving this way again? You know we go on this trip every year. Why do you have to make this so hard? I want to see my family, and I want you to go. But, frankly, at this point, it would be fine if you just stayed home."

Shocked that the bold truth of bad behavior has been unveiled, our peevish partner retreats to consider the next move.

DIG and Your Elemental Style

Not every couple is cut out for doing the laundry together. While you may like the way your partner dresses, when it comes to doing the dirty work, it just isn't going to wash out.

Your elemental style gives you insight into your deeper needs and explains the nature of your DIG work. Knowing what you and your partner need to work on improves your ability to get along.

Your elemental style also reveals specific abilities that allow you to work it out with your partner. These abilities are like the detergent that changes dirty to clean, enabling you to make better choices, chose different actions, and resolve problems in a healthier way.

In subsequent chapters, we'll talk more about each of these specific abilities. For now, they are listed below. At this point, let's just say that knowing your elemental style creates an individual method for inner growth.

ELEMENTAL ABILITIES: THE LAUNDRY DETERGENT OF DIG			
FIRE	AIR	WATER	EARTH
Humility	Focus	Trust	Flexibility
Gentleness	Sensitivity	Restraint	Charity

Dr. Craig Martin

If you want to change, you need to be patient.
Honest self-reflection takes time.

Introspection and Feeling Safe

Confrontation and observation do not always go smoothly. Often they make you feel vulnerable. Vulnerability can make you feel unsafe. When you're confronted, feelings of guilt, shame, inadequacy, imperfection, stupidity, or unworthiness can result, and none of these are any fun. It's important to have someone you feel comfortable with. Your laundry is a private matter, and you won't feel safe showing it to just anyone. Most often, DIG occurs in a safe environment. So to share yourself with someone else, you need to feel safe with that person.

If you want to change, you need to be patient. Honest self-reflection takes time. After all, you can't finish the laundry in an hour, and there's always more laundry to do. One change leads to the next.

So besides knowing what you need to work on and having a partner who wants to work on it with you, you need patience. Even learning how to do the laundry correctly takes time. What temperature do you use? How do you separate colors? What detergent works best? DIG takes practice to get it right.

Time is needed to develop intimacy skills and find out what a safe environment for introspection means to you. This would be your laundry room. In upcoming chapters, you'll find specific examples of safe space for each elemental style. When you have the right space for self-reflection, you'll be able to figure out what needs a little extra scrubbing.

A DIG Story, Part 2: Time to Self-Reflect

Our cranky, but very lovable, reluctant traveler is off licking the wounds of confrontation.

Ouch! Am I really that difficult when it comes to visiting my in-laws? No, it's just that I really don't like going up there. But I'm not going to stay home. That would be really unfair. We always go together to visit my family. So I really need to do this. But, wow, I really don't like it.

Maybe I am being that difficult. That would be really uncool. Is there any way I can go and not make it a nightmare for my partner or me? Maybe. I'll have to think about it.

Self-Discovery

Introspection may lead you to see things about yourself that are not so attractive. The dirty laundry never is. Sometimes you may want to pick it up with two fingers and turn your face away. Sometimes you wish the dirty clothes would fly into the washing machine without your having to touch them at all. Don't despair. Everyone else has dirty laundry. The trick is realizing that the longer it's left unattended, the worse it gets. Ignoring the laundry could get really ugly, just like ignoring your laundry list.

Self-reflection is a personal process that you do for yourself. When you clean your dirty laundry, you don't do it for your partner. You do it for yourself. You're the one who wants to feel clean, and it makes you feel good.

Getting rid of the negative stuff is not easy, but it makes you feel better about yourself. The benefits far outweigh the effort. You get to live as your better self and enjoy a truly meaningful relationship with your partner. So embrace the process.

Acceptance and Allowance

After doing a bit of self-reflection, you might decide that you can reject the difficult parts of yourself. Instead of washing your dirty clothes, you could throw them away and buy new ones. But that approach wouldn't last long.

You can't take all the things in your personality that need work, stuff them in a box, and shove them in the back of the closet. You can't write down your personality traits on a sheet of paper, good stuff on the left, bad stuff on the right, rip the paper in half, and throw the bad stuff away.

These qualities, the good and the bad, are who you are. You cannot just eliminate your less-desirable self. So why not accept it? Then you can work to change what you don't like. When you fully accept yourself, you can manage the harder qualities. By allowing yourself to be a complete person, the good parts along with the bad, you gain a greater ability to change. You can't really do the laundry until you admit that it needs to be done. This goes along with self-honesty.

A DIG Story, Part 3: Resolution

Later the same day, a whole new person shows up for the trip. Realizing that sulking and tantrums are manipulation, our reformed partner is ready to go see the in-laws. "You know, I just want to feel that you understand why this is hard for me."

To which comes the reply, "Well, that's no problem. Please, do you think this is a picnic for me?"

And they drive off laughing.

Choosing the Negative and Coming Clean

At some point, DIG leads you to realize that you've been acting badly. You sit with some aspect of yourself and see your fault in a situation. When you had to decide between your positive and negative sides, you chose the negative route.

Well, that's okay. We all choose the negative path sometimes. When we admit it to ourselves—wow—that's when real DIG can happen. Really taking a look at yourself is hard. Honesty and accountability are scary sometimes and a bit nerve-wracking. But with practice, you get better at it. Intimacy is a skill; as you improve that skill, you improve your relationship.

Apology and Forgiveness

All this self-reflection and change for the better must have resulted in clean laundry by now, right? Well, yes, and it might be a good time to apologize if your dirty laundry was making things a mess. Maybe you chose to act from the negative part of your character. Putting your dirty laundry out there can be unpleasant. Is an apology in order? Or maybe it's time to accept your partner's apology and forgive them. Apology and forgiveness definitely follow DIG.

The Cycle of Self-Improvement

Intimacy is a positive cycle, a beautiful process that results in self-improvement. This positive cycle of self-improvement serves to deepen your relationship and make it more authentic, more connected, and more fun. You really get to know each other.

The outworn way of doing things includes self-righteousness—that is, the belief that you're right all the time. Self-righteousness leads to denial, which leads to defensiveness and then blame, where anything that's wrong in the relationship must be your partner's fault. This is the negative cycle of creating distance in your relationship, the opposite of intimacy. DIG can transform the negative cycle into the positive one.

The chart on the next page illustrates how DIG transforms the negative cycle of distance in your relationship into a positive cycle of connection and intimacy.

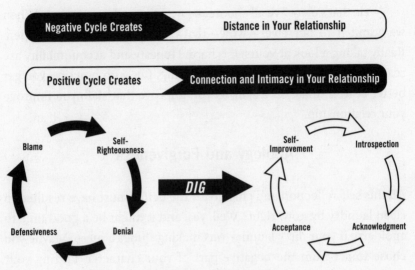

| Negative Cycle Creates | Distance in Your Relationship |
| Positive Cycle Creates | Connection and Intimacy in Your Relationship |

The chart above illustrates how DIG transforms the negative cycle
of distance in your relationship into a positive cycle
of connection and intimacy.

In the process of getting to know yourself, you develop a strong
conscience, which is another word for self-honesty. Your conscience
helps you interact with your partner in a meaningful way. Instead of
hiding the laundry, you open up, allow yourself to feel vulnerable,
and work it out. All that work and DIG leads to a healthy and honest
relationship.

The Three Gifts of DIG

DIG has three benefits. They are earned through introspection,
honesty, and your attempt to change for the better.

1. Self-understanding: Knowing who you are allows you to face
yourself in a relationship. The more you know yourself, the less
chance you will be shocked by what your partner sees. Self-

understanding creates the foundation for working it out with someone.

2. Forgiveness: By realizing that you're not perfect, you can forgive others more easily. They're not perfect either, and that's okay. Relationships can't last without forgiveness. Your partner will upset you, and you will upset your partner. Forgiving yourself and each other is essential.

3. Compromise: Relationships are a give and take or, better yet, a give and accept. To get, you have to give. Through your willingness to compromise, you acknowledge that your partner has needs too. Most human interactions require some compromise. DIG gets you in touch with your complete self so that you can compromise your position without giving up your values.

It is a given that relationships are fun, passionate, and exciting. Those things don't usually trip up your interactions with your partner. It's the lack of awareness that often causes relationship difficulties. DIG is the way to create self-awareness and clear up misunderstandings.

The next four chapters describe how your elemental style does the laundry—that is, how to work with the complete you, do the DIG work for your style, and come out squeaky clean!

9
Fire Works It Out

Fire style has the big ideas. You also have the passion and energy to push your ideas out in front. Fire folks want to win. That's because you're certain your approach to any situation is the right approach. You have a pretty high opinion of your opinion.

Fire needs

- To feel important
- To be in control and in charge
- To have things go their way
- To win

From chapter 3, you may remember that Fire's positive qualities include being original, enthusiastic, and motivational. These basic traits form the basis for Fire's needs. If you weren't so important, why in the world would anyone pay attention to your amazing ideas in the first place?

Your need to feel important and in control originates from your position as the creative one. Fire people are bursting with ideas, and you really want to be noticed for your creativity. You need to be in control to express your ideas. If people don't recognize your ideas, then someone else's ideas will get the spotlight. To you, that's just unacceptable, and it explains why Fire needs control.

Fire's Choice

Most of the time when Fire-style people try to get what they need, they act from their positive qualities. But what happens when you don't feel in control? What happens when situations arise that cause you to feel unnoticed? That's when you come up against Fire's choice, the decision to act from the positive or negative part of your personality. You choose to create a sense of importance through motivation and kindness or intimidation and demands.

When we get our first glimpse of the Great and Powerful Oz in *The Wizard of Oz*, he is a disembodied head surrounded by flames. He roars, "Go away," as he calls out commands and orders.

Oz, at first, is an image of Fire choosing to intimidate others. He is afraid that people won't feel he's important. Perhaps he doesn't feel big enough just as he is. So he inflates his worth through fear and dominance. He gets what he wants—importance and awe—but in the process he alienates the very people who might admire him.

Fire makes the same choice when not in control and not winning. Somewhere inside, you say to yourself, "I don't feel in control right now, so I'm going to act in a domineering manner to get what I need." Often, this happens without your even realizing it. You could be totally unaware of your motives. You just want to get your needs met. You simply act domineering to feel in control or because you want to get your way. Fire chooses to act out in a negative way when feeling vulnerable.

Fire and Vulnerability

Fire feels vulnerable when

- They're not the center of attention
- Others make decisions for them
- They can't get their way
- They lose

To show how Fire feels vulnerable, I'd like to explore a simple scene between two people. Joe is our Fire-style person, and Mary is his partner. Joe sits down to dinner, and he needs to feel important. He's the man of the house, after all. The external exchanges between Joe and Mary are in the left column. Their internal drama is included on the right.

EXTERNAL EXCHANGES WHAT'S HAPPENING	INTERNAL DRAMA WHAT'S REALLY GOING ON
Joe: PASS THE SALT!	He gives an order. He's had a hard day at work.
Mary: What do you mean, "PASS THE SALT"? Who do you think I am? Your waitress?	She confronts him. She's had a hard day too.
Joe: No, but you're just sitting there. You're my partner. Don't give me a hard time. Just pass it over here already.	He **defends** himself and becomes intimidating. When he doesn't get his way, he feels vulnerable. He begins to choose the negative path.
Mary: Well, I wish you would stop giving me orders. You didn't say "please." You don't even say "thank you" when I pass you the salt!	She gets more confrontational. She feels that she really needs to set this boundary.

Continued on next page

Continued from previous page

EXTERNAL EXCHANGES WHAT'S HAPPENING	INTERNAL DRAMA WHAT'S REALLY GOING ON
Joe: I do too! You're just being hypersensitive.	He **blames** her.
Mary: Don't push this off on me. I'm not being hypersensitive.	She confronts him again, refusing to take the blame.
Joe: Well, you're making this up. I didn't even talk down to you. I just said, "Pass the salt." Stop making a big deal out of nothing.	He goes into **denial**. He still refuses to accept responsibility.
Mary: Joe, you didn't just say, "Pass the salt." You said, "PASS THE SALT!" It was your tone.	She tries once again to get him to see that he might have overstepped her boundaries.
Joe: No, I didn't.	He shows his complete lack of accountability.
Mary: Well, guess what. We're out of salt.	It ends. She's hurt and feels vulnerable too.

This example is just one of the many possible conflicts that can result when Fire feels vulnerable. Maybe it started before Joe even came home. Maybe he didn't feel important or get his way at work. So when he came home, he was already feeling the negative side of Fire. Then when he didn't get his way at home, he felt vulnerable. He became defensive and acted in an intimidating manner.

Fire people also feel vulnerable when others don't offer recognition or when others are in charge of making decisions. The scenarios are many, but the outcomes are the same: when Fire-style individuals feel vulnerable, they get defensive. Let's look at how.

Defending Yourself

Oz defends his need to feel important by intimidating those around him. Rather than choose the good side of Fire, he tries to achieve superiority through forcefulness. This is part of Fire's defense.

As a defense, Fire-style people demand obedience,
forcing their ideas onto others and insisting on compliance.
In this way, Fire can take credit for everything
that happens around them.

When Fire feels vulnerable, other defensive qualities surface, including being accusatory, righteous, and combative. Fire people use these behaviors to ensure that they are always right and never wrong. That's the negative way Fire achieves importance. When a Fire person's deeper needs are unfulfilled, he or she can become defensive.

Defense for Fire: Fire's dirty laundry
- Intimidation
- Accusation
- Righteousness
- Combativeness

All our negative qualities are defenses, and defensiveness is where dynamic inner growth (DIG) work comes into play. As a Fire-style person, ask yourself, "Am I intimidating?" "Am I overpowering?" and "Am I bossy?" If you answered yes to any of these and would like to change, it's time for Fire's DIG. Onward!

Working It Out: How DIG Work Occurs in Fire

DIG begins when you look at your part in a disagreement. For Fire style, the questions are, "Was I kind or intimidating?" and "Did I overpower or

PERSONAL DRIVES	BEHAVIOR WHEN VULNERABLE	DIG WORK ABILITIES	BEHAVIOR AFTER DIG WORK
Self-importance	Arrogant	Humility	Generous
Control	Forceful	Gentleness	Kind
Dominance	Accusatory		Motivating
	Demanding		Inspiring

persuade?" If you chose to intimidate or overpower, you need to look within and admit what you did. You can do that with humility and gentleness, the abilities that enable Fire to experience DIG.

Let's check in on Joe and Mary again (see dialogue on the following page). This time, Mary is the Fire style. Joe's getting ready to mow the lawn, but Mary has other plans.

The choice for Mary is to meet her needs through demands and intimidation or through understanding and kindness. Her willingness to do the DIG work of Fire style makes the difference. Humility and gentleness are the foundation of that work. You need these abilities to change negative expressions into positive ones.

Humility is the ability to admit that you may be wrong or that somebody else may be right. It is the ability to say, "I'm sorry." Can you do that, Fire? Of course you can! With Joe and the salt, he could stop and ask himself, "Was I talking down to her?" If he's honest, Joe will realize that he chose to act in a demanding and domineering way.

Humility is also about listening. If your words are domineering and accusatory, it's unlikely that you're listening to your partner. Recognize that someone besides you might have something important to say. As you can see, Fire sometimes needs to work on humility.

You also need gentleness, which is the ability to go easy and understand that you don't have to overpower or frighten someone to

EXTERNAL EXCHANGES WHAT'S HAPPENING	INTERNAL DRAMA WHAT'S REALLY GOING ON
Mary: Today we're going to visit my mother!	She takes charge, making a statement of fact without even asking.
Joe: Oh, okay. But I thought I was going to do the yard work today.	He tries to set a boundary.
Mary: Well, you thought wrong. We're visiting my mother today.	She **ups the ante**. This makes her statement sound even more controlling and demanding.
Joe: It really wasn't on my agenda. Can we go tomorrow? It's going to rain tomorrow. I should do the lawn today.	He confronts her, stating his truth and trying to stand in it.
Mary: I told you I wanted to go today. Why didn't you do the lawn before now?	She becomes **accusatory** and **intimidating**. These are her ways of defending herself.
Joe: Well, because you didn't actually tell me, so I wasn't able to plan for that. If I had known, I'd have done it earlier.	He restates his truth and, at the same time, gives her what she needs. He validates her importance. He's not just giving her a hard time for the fun of it.
Mary: All right, I guess that's true. Sorry. I'll make you some iced tea. It's hot outside.	She really just wanted to feel important. When she does her DIG work, she is gentle and can change from negative to positive behavior.
Joe: You're the best!	He loves her for her Fire style!

get your way. You could just as easily coax your partner. Why not put that amazing creativity to good use and try gentleness?

Humility and gentleness are the way Fire digs. Together, these abilities help Fire individuals confront their need for importance and realize that a situation may not revolve around them and isn't won by intimidation.

Own It, Admit It, Be in Touch with It

After working on his DIG, the Wizard of Oz chooses the best part of Fire. He makes the choice to act with benevolence. In the final scene, he grants Dorothy and her companions their requests. Instead of intimidation, Oz uses his creativity to give gifts and answer the needs of Dorothy and her friends.

For Fire-style Oz, kindness and generosity prevail as he realizes that people hold him in awe because of his big heart and not because he's frightening. He offers to share his balloon to help Dorothy get home, and, through the process of confrontation and self-reflection, transforms himself. He confronts his negative trait of intimidation and embraces Fire's kindness. The Wizard of Oz shows the dynamic inner growth of Fire.

If Fire is your style, you can make a choice to look at Fire's laundry list and come clean. In the process, domination can turn into leadership and bossiness can become motivational. Which type of person would you rather have for a partner?

Fire's Time for Introspection

Finding the right time for self-reflection is essential. Fire's safe space for DIG work is in things that create personal challenge. Of course, you can introspect anytime and anywhere, but when you feel like a winner, you will grow from a positive place. By putting yourself in circumstances where you meet your own needs, you create an environment that's free from defensiveness. It is here that you can do your self-reflective DIG work.

Fire can have a positive inner growth experience through sports, crafts, and nature. Any place you can challenge yourself, improve, create, and excel is a good place to self-reflect.

You'll want to look for humility and gentleness, and the best place is where you're the best. Try to set up a personal challenge. Just pick anything you're good at. Climb another mountain, but go higher this time. Go out on the golf course by yourself, hit a few balls, and reflect on your good score and your need for importance and humility. If you like to knit, try learning a more difficult stitch. In those hours working with the knitting needles, think about gentleness and how it could improve your relationship.

Maybe it wouldn't be too much sweat off your back if you went for a hike and realized that you *could* meet your partner's desire to hear "please" a little more often. You can discover many good things in the safety of Fire's environment for introspection.

Fire's activities for introspection
- Crafts
- Sports
- Personal challenge
- Nature

Fire Apologizes

When you finally—and I mean finally—admit to yourself that you were wrong—and, oh, how you loathe that word—you will apologize in the grandest of ways. Compliments fly.

Surprise gifts are likely in store, and generous gifts at that. Your partner will enjoy your expansive generosity, creativity, support, and gentleness. It actually feels good to apologize, though you might never admit it.

Fire expresses an apology by offering
- Compliments
- Surprises
- Generosity
- Support

Questions for Self-Awareness

The following questions might lead you to some good discussions with yourself, a friend, or your lover. These are Fire's questions for self-reflection and DIG.

1. Could I be kinder, more generous, or more benevolent right now on any level—with my mind, my inner judgments, my words, or my actions? Could I be more generous to the person I am having a conflict with?
2. If I am making demands right now, could I compromise and still get my needs met?
3. Why do I want a relationship if everything is always about me?
4. Am I accusing someone without all the facts or without listening?
5. Do I always have to be right? How would it feel if I didn't have to be right all the time?
6. Does my desire for adoration make me afraid to hear what my partner really thinks?

Fire's mantra: I can go easy; I go easy.

Whom Fire Needs

To DIG into your stuff, you will need someone who can handle your demanding and self-focused ways. Most of all, you need someone who lets you take charge. (Not all the time, obviously.) For you, it would be too competitive or disappointing if you didn't have a lot of space to make decisions in the relationship.

It's no surprise that your partner finds you fascinating, especially your creativity and larger-than-life personality. But your partner has to accommodate your take-charge attitude and constant need for praise, or your needs will not be met. You need to feel important in the relationship, and you thrive on your partner's admiration. If your partner understands these things about you and gives you what you need, the relationship can thrive.

DIG Work for Fire

The chart below shows how Fire in nature can be difficult to cope with and destructive when expressed in an uncontrolled way. The corresponding DIG qualities are shown as well. These are the traits you need to work on if Fire style is your elemental type.

FIRE IN NATURE NEGATIVE ATTRIBUTES	YOUR FIERY NATURE DIG WORK QUALITIES
Burning	Self-righteous, egotistical, accusatory, arrogant
Destructive	Domineering, aggressive, combative, prejudiced
Uncontrolled	Boastful, pushy, haughty
Scorching	Audacious, pompous
Overpowering	Argumentative, bossy, severe, temperamental, exaggerating
Smoldering	Obstinate, intolerant, quarrelsome

10
Air Works It Out

Air style is exemplified by the communicator. You are the talker, the reader, and the teacher. Air-style people want to be free thinkers. That's because your mind is your sacred temple of truth. You think an accurate and precise choice of words is of indubitable importance.

Air needs
- To feel mentally stimulated
- To be free
- To have personal space
- To think

From chapter 4, you may remember that Air's positive qualities include independence, inquisitiveness, and fair-mindedness. These traits form the basis for Air's needs. As an independent thinker, you are the one in charge of keeping your mind active and your conclusions free from bias.

Your need to feel unrestricted and stimulated originates from your position as the thinker. Air people have really busy, curious minds, and you want space to mentally explore. This helps you discover the truth. You need the freedom to think for yourself. Otherwise, someone else's thinking could confuse you, and that's just unacceptable. Your intelligence depends on making sure that everything is clearly understood.

Air's Choice

Most of the time when Air-style people try to get what they need, they act from their positive qualities. But what happens when you don't feel well informed? What happens when situations arise that cause you to feel restricted or boxed in? That's when you come up against Air's choice, the decision to act from the positive or negative part of your personality. You choose to create freedom of thought by staying attentive and focused or by becoming scattered and dismissive.

As the White Rabbit races along in *Alice in Wonderland*, this much is clear: He's late! He's this. He's that. He's busy. He's anything but centered, focused, or relaxed. He's all over the place. He has paperwork, scrolls, trumpets, and a packed agenda. The White Rabbit really has a lot going on—so many things, in fact, that he's overwhelmed and short-circuiting. But the real problem is that he's preoccupied with getting to the court on time. He is so distracted that he can't focus on anything else—certainly not on Alice and her problem. By choosing to act in a scattered and dismissive manner, he cannot be pinned down and thus meets his need for freedom by expressing his negative qualities.

The White Rabbit, at first, is a picture of Air choosing negative behavior qualities. If he doesn't keep all his responsibilities in check, he will pay with his head. Ouch! Perhaps he's so overwhelmed that he's not capable of focusing. So he meets his need for mental stimulation by behaving in a way that's high-strung, distracted, and preoccupied. He gets what he wants—freedom and space—but misses out on Alice, the very person who might provide him with new and interesting knowledge and mental stimulation.

Air's choice also originates from feeling restricted or stifled. Somewhere inside, you say to yourself, "I can't think straight, so I'm going to excuse myself from focusing on you to get what I need." Often, this happens without your even realizing it. You could remain totally unaware of your motives. You just want to get your needs met. You simply act in a dismissive manner to feel unrestricted or because you need space to think. Air chooses to act out in a negative way when feeling vulnerable.

Air and Vulnerability

Air feels vulnerable when

- Focusing for long periods
- Feeling restricted
- In an emotionally heavy situation
- Overwhelmed and can't think

To show how Air feels vulnerable, I'd like to explore a simple scene where Air is dismissive (see dialogue on the following page). John is our Air-style person, and Sue is his partner. Sue walks into the room and wants to share her day, but John needs space. He wants time for himself. The external exchanges between John and Sue are in the left column. Their internal drama is included on the right.

This example is just one of the many possible conflicts that can result when Air feels vulnerable. Perhaps it started before Sue even walked in the door. Maybe John was feeling overwhelmed and didn't have any more space left for her. So when Sue walks into the room, he's already preoccupied, distant, and expressing the negative side of Air. Then when she wants more from him, he feels vulnerable. He becomes defensive and dismissive.

EXTERNAL EXCHANGES WHAT'S HAPPENING	INTERNAL DRAMA WHAT'S REALLY GOING ON
Sue: Honey, I'm home!	She hopes to get his attention.
(John doesn't answer. He's reading the newspaper.)	He is preoccupied with his own interests.
Sue: Honey? I'm home. Can I get a minute to tell you what happened at work today?	She asks him for what she needs.
John: Right. What? (He doesn't look up from what he's doing.)	He's dismissive of her needs.
Sue: Come on, John! Why won't you look up from what you're doing? I'm talking to you.	She confronts him. She really wants him to listen to her.
John: I said, "What?" What else do you want from me?	He **defends** himself and becomes insensitive. When he feels restricted, he gets vulnerable. He begins to choose the negative path.
Sue: Well, I wish you would stop for a second and give me the time of day. I feel like you don't even care about what I have to say at all.	She gets more confrontational. She feels that she really needs to set this boundary.
John: That's not true. You're just being demanding.	He **blames** her.
Sue: No, I'm not. I just want to tell you about my day.	She confronts him again, refusing to take the blame.
John: Fine! Look! I'm listening. Okay?! (He continues to read the paper and tunes out.)	He goes into **denial**. He shows his complete lack of accountability.
Sue: Great. Thanks. I'm going to call my mother.	It ends. She's hurt and feeling vulnerable too.

Air people also feel vulnerable if they need to focus for too long on one thing or if a situation gets too emotionally heavy. The scenarios are many, but the outcomes are the same: when Air-style individuals feel vulnerable, they get defensive. Let's look at how.

Defending Yourself

The White Rabbit defends his need for mental stimulation by acting scattered. Rather than choose the good side of Air, he maintains his freedom by making sure he's too busy for anything else. This is a part of Air-style defense.

> *As a defense, Air-style people spin the truth, creating convincing little twists to the tale of their own realities. In this way, Air remains blameless for everything that happens around them.*

When Air feels vulnerable, other defensive qualities surface, including indifference, dismissiveness, avoidance, and insensitivity. Air people use these behaviors to ensure that they feel unhindered. That's the negative way Air attains space and independence. When an Air person's deeper needs are unfulfilled, he or she becomes defensive.

Defense for Air: Air's dirty laundry
- Scattered
- Avoidant
- Dismissive
- Insensitive

Our negative qualities are defenses, and defensiveness is where dynamic inner growth (DIG) work comes into play. As an Air-style person, ask yourself, "Am I scattered?" "Am I avoiding someone or something?" "Am I insensitive?" If you answered yes to any of these questions and would like to change, it's time for Air's DIG. Forward!

Working It Out: How DIG Work Occurs in Air

PERSONAL DRIVES	BEHAVIOR WHEN VULNERABLE	DIG WORK ABILITIES	BEHAVIOR AFTER DIG WORK
Truth	Dismissive	Sensitivity	Communicative
Freedom	Scattered	Focus	Adaptable
Mental stimulation	Indifferent		Witty
	Insensitive		Diplomatic

DIG begins when you look at your part in a disagreement. For Air style, the questions are, "Was I attentive or dismissive?" "Was I indifferent or present?" If you chose dismissiveness or indifference, you need to look within and recognize what you did. You can do that with sensitivity and focus, the abilities that enable Air to experience DIG.

Let's check in on John and Sue again (see dialogue on the following page). This time, Sue is the Air style. John and Sue are on their way back from vacation. After several hours of driving, they get off the road to find a place to eat.

The choice for Sue is to meet her needs by acting in an impatient and dismissive manner or by showing patience and involvement. Her willingness to do the DIG work of Air style is what makes the difference. Sensitivity and focus are the foundation of that work. You need these abilities to change negative expressions into positive ones.

Sensitivity is the ability to see beyond logic. It allows you to understand that other people have feelings and recognize that words

EXTERNAL EXCHANGES WHAT'S HAPPENING	INTERNAL DRAMA WHAT'S REALLY GOING ON
John: I'm hungry. Let's get off the highway here and find someplace nice to eat.	He expresses his needs.
Sue: Okay, but let's make it snappy. I want to get home soon.	She minimizes his needs by suggesting that they hurry.
John: Snappy? I was thinking that we could find someplace nice. This is the last night of our vacation.	He elaborates and asks again if she can meet his needs.
Sue: Well, fast food is fine with me. Let's not waste time. This is such a bother.	She **ups the ante**. This makes her statement even more dismissive and insensitive.
John: Fast food?! This is our last night of vacation, and you want fast food? I want to sit down for dinner in some nice surroundings. It could be romantic.	He confronts her, stating his truth and trying to stand in it.
Sue: You're taking too long, and I want to go home. Right now I don't care about your romantic dinner!	She becomes even more **insensitive**. This is how she defends herself. But she also reveals her needs.
John: Well, I do! And I know we can find the right place in no time. (Just moments later, he turns and finds the perfect place.)	He restates his truth and, at the same time, gives her what she needs. He validates her need to keep moving. He's not looking to give her a hard time.
Sue: All right, I guess you were right. I'm sorry. It looks like we might have a nice time here. Thanks for finding it so quickly.	She really just wanted to feel unrestricted. When she does her DIG work, she can change from negative to positive behavior.
John: You're the best!	He loves her for her Air style!

can hurt. Can you imagine that, Air? Of course you can! With John and the newspaper, he could stop and ask himself, "Was I ignoring

Sue?" If he's honest, John will realize that he chose to act in an insensitive and distant way.

Sensitivity also involves caring about someone else's pain, discomfort, or fear. Try to realize that another person might need a bit of your focus and attention, and might actually deserve it. As you can see, Air sometimes needs to work on sensitivity.

You also need focus, which is the ability to stay on target and follow through. When you are focused, you stay in the moment and don't move on to something new as soon as you feel confined. Why not put that amazing mind to good use and try focusing it?

Sensitivity and focus are the ways that Air digs. Together, these abilities help Air individuals confront their need for mental stimulation and freedom. Then Air doesn't have to handle emotional situations with distance but can offer attention and sensitivity.

Own It, Admit It, Be in Touch with It

After working on his DIG, the White Rabbit chooses the best part of Air. He makes the choice to remain present and act with fairness. In the final scene, when Alice is on trial for nonsensical crimes, the White Rabbit speaks up for her, saying that her treatment is unjust.

For the Air-style White Rabbit, truth and justice prevail as he criticizes the King of Hearts, not once but twice. The King of Hearts is the supposed judge, but the Queen of Hearts is waiting to dispense the sentence.

At the risk of losing his head, the White Rabbit says and then repeats, "We can't pass the sentence before we hear the evidence." Using logic and diplomacy, he points out that the court is behaving illogically. Through the process of self-reflection, the White Rabbit transforms himself. He confronts his negative behavior of acting scattered and dismissive and embraces his positive traits of focus and attentiveness.

If Air is your style, you can make a choice to look at Air's laundry list and come clean. In the process, insensitivity can turn into fairness and distraction can become focus. Which type of person would you rather have for a partner?

Air's Time for Introspection

Finding the right time for self-reflection is essential. Air's safe place for DIG work is whatever encourages an inner dialogue. Of course, you can introspect anytime and anywhere, but when you feel mentally engaged, you will grow from a positive place. By putting yourself in circumstances where you are meeting your own needs, you will create an environment that's free from defensiveness. It is here that you can do your self-reflective DIG work.

Air can achieve positive inner growth through journal writing, reading, affirmations, and laughter. Any activity that allows Air to think, communicate, and act lighthearted provides a place and time for self-reflection.

You'll want to look at sensitivity and focus. The best way to do that is with thought-provoking actions. Try writing in a journal. Perhaps call your journal "Thoughts on Dynamic Inner Growth" or "I'd Cry If I Weren't So Busy Laughing." Try setting up a daily affirmation calendar with entries such as "Today I will listen" or "Today I will practice focus." If you like to read, maybe you can pick up something that puts your mind at ease. That might create a space for you to think about how you had recently acted with your partner, rather than ignoring what happened and hoping that the issue won't come up again.

Maybe you could watch a comedy, laugh a little, and give yourself some space to think. As you reflect on your relationship, you might decide that it's important to make more time for your partner. You can discover many good things in the safety of Air's time for introspection.

Air's activities for introspection

- Journaling
- Reading
- Affirmations
- Laughing

Air Apologizes

When you apologize, it's usually after you've thought about it for some time. Air is keen on justice, so when you think you're at fault, you will fess up. So get out your pen or keyboard, because if "I'm sorry" can be said in two words, a thousand words can say it better. When you want forgiveness, emails, letters, and phone calls are in order. Your elaborate way with words will come in handy as you tell your partner all you did wrong in the most effusive and honest way.

Air expresses an apology through

- Emails
- Letters
- Phone calls
- Talking

Questions for Self-Awareness

The following questions might lead you to some good discussions with yourself, a friend, or your lover. These are Air's questions for self-reflection and DIG.

1. Could I be more focused in my day-to-day life or see my distractions for what they really are? If so, how?
2. What would happen if I connected more deeply with this person whom I like or love?

3. This person is important to me, right? So why did I just turn away or turn off so quickly?
4. How would it feel to completely follow through?
5. Do I always have to make light of everything or never allow myself to be completely serious by making a joke out of everything?
6. Does my desire for freedom make me afraid to listen to my partner's feelings and concerns?

Air's mantra: I can see clearly; I see clearly.

Whom Air Needs

To DIG into your stuff, you will need someone who can handle your talkativeness and scattered behavior. Most of all, you need someone who gives you space and freedom. (Not all the time, obviously.) But you can find life boring or confining when you don't have space to talk out loud and just act ditsy every now and then.

Your partner is probably fascinated by your intelligence and quick wit. But your partner has to accommodate your need for independence and space, or your needs will not be met. You need to feel stimulated in the relationship and love your partner's mind as well. If your partner understands these things about you and gives you what you need, this relationship will be a real meeting of the minds and hearts.

DIG Work for Air

The chart on the following page shows how Air in nature can be difficult to cope with and chilly when expressed in a negative way. The corresponding DIG qualities are shown as well. These are the traits you will want to work on if Air style is your elemental type.

AIR IN NATURE NEGATIVE ATTRIBUTES	YOUR AIRY NATURE DIG WORK QUALITIES
Foggy	Distracted, insensitive, dismissive
Chilly	Cold, aloof, cynical, critical
Polluted	Bitter, devious, unfair
Suffocating	High-strung, meddlesome, nervous, narrow-minded
Hazy	Unreliable, inconstant, superficial
Stale	Vain, self-pitying

11
Water Works It Out

Water style is the feelings style. You live in the realm of moods, sensations, and intuition. Water people want to trust their emotions. That's because you sense the truth rather than think it. It's not always easy to find validation for your perceptiveness in a world of logic and proof.

What water needs
- To feel emotionally validated
- To be understood
- To have reassurances
- To trust

From chapter 5, you may recall that Water's positive qualities include being imaginative, artistic, and compassionate. These traits form the basis for Water's needs. Expressing your deep sensitivity to the world feels so much better when someone understands where you're coming from.

Your need to feel emotionally validated and reassured originates from your position as the transforming one. Water takes ideas and changes them. These changes are based on your feelings. Water people will alter something so that it fits within their framework of what feels right. Without your sensitivity and insight, life would lack understanding and depth, which is just unacceptable and why Water people need others to validate their feelings.

Water's Choice

Most of the time when Water-style people try to get what they need, they act from their positive qualities. But what happens when you don't feel emotionally validated? What happens when situations arise that cause you to feel misunderstood and distrustful? That's when you come up against Water's choice, the decision to act from the positive or negative part of your personality. You choose to create emotional validation either through affection and compassion or manipulation and martyrdom.

Tinkerbell, the fairy in *Peter Pan*, is an artist. She gets her name because she likes to experiment, make things, and tinker with metal. Tinkerbell represents imagination, and she is very protective of Peter and the boys, so much so that when Wendy comes on the scene, Tinkerbell is filled with jealousy and contempt. To rid herself of this emotional rival, she aids Captain Hook in Wendy's capture.

Tinkerbell becomes a picture of Water choosing manipulation. Her scorn, created by Peter's affection for Wendy, brings out the worst in her. She thinks that if she can eliminate Wendy, she will gain the emotional connection she needs. Perhaps she doesn't see that Peter can hold a special place for her even while enjoying the company of his new friend. So Tinkerbell meets her need for emotional validation by acting in a resentful, spoiled, and revengeful manner. At first, she gets what she wants—Peter all to herself—but it's a false attachment that causes her to miss out on any real connection.

Water's choice also occurs when you feel misunderstood or distrustful. Somewhere inside, you say, "I don't feel that you understand me, so I'm going to manipulate you to get what I need." Often, this happens without your even realizing it. You could remain totally unaware of your motives. You just want to get your needs met. You manipulate to feel emotionally understood or because you need someone to feel the way you feel. So Water chooses to act out in a negative way when feeling vulnerable.

Water and Vulnerability

Water feels vulnerable when
- Disconnected from others
- Misunderstood emotionally
- Uncared for by people they love
- Distrustful

To show how Water feels vulnerable, I'd like to explore a simple scene between two people, in which Water tries to manipulate (see dialogue on the following page). Bill is our Water-style person, and Sam is his partner. It's Bill's birthday. Sam has just given him a gift but no card. The external exchanges between Bill and Sam are in the left column. Their internal drama is included on the right.

This example is just one of the many possible conflicts that can result when Water feels vulnerable. Maybe it started before Sam even gave Bill the present. Maybe Bill hadn't received any cards in the mail because deliveries were late. So when he gets the present from Sam, he is already moody, resentful, and expressing the negative side of Water. When he doesn't get the desired validation from Sam, he feels vulnerable. That leads him to become defensive and act like a martyr.

EXTERNAL EXCHANGES WHAT'S HAPPENING	INTERNAL DRAMA WHAT'S REALLY GOING ON
Sam: Happy birthday, honey!	He has really put some thought into this year's gift.
Bill: Gee … um … thanks, but was there a card with this, honey? I didn't see one.	Rather than focus on what he received, Bill starts to feel hurt because his emotional needs aren't satisfied.
Sam: Oh, I'm sorry. I meant to pick one up, but I ran out of time. Open it! Open it!	He tries to make light of it and move on.
Bill: Wow, I'd really like to get a card. I can't believe you didn't get a card.	He begins to manipulate the situation using guilt or a sense of duty.
Sam: I know, but I spent a lot of time on your present. Isn't that enough?	He feels that he tried his best.
Bill: No, actually it's not. Buying something is easy. I really like it when you write something. I thought you knew me by now.	He gets **defensive**. He feels uncared for and emotionally misunderstood. He begins to choose the negative path.
Sam: Well, I didn't know. I'll go buy you a card right now, if you want.	He tries again to make it better.
Bill: Don't bother. It's too late now. You ruined it already.	He **blames** him.
Sam: I didn't ruin anything. I got you a great gift actually. You're ruining it for yourself.	He defends himself, refusing to take the blame.
Bill: Right, I forgot to get myself a card. I'll run out now and get one.	His sarcasm shows how hurt he feels and how unwilling he is to accept the situation.
Sam: Why don't you?!	It ends. Sam is hurt and feeling vulnerable too.

Water individuals can also feel vulnerable when emotionally disconnected from others or if they lose trust in people. The scenarios are many, but the outcomes are the same: when Water-style people feel vulnerable, they get defensive. Let's look at how.

Defending Yourself

Tinkerbell defends her emotional needs by acting in manipulative ways. Rather than choose the good side of Water, she maintains her connection to Peter by behaving in a jealous and deceptive manner. This is part of Water-style defense.

> *As a defense, Water-style people manipulate the emotions of others, using guilt and a sense of duty to create their own emotional stability. In this way, Water deflects responsibility for their feelings and everything that happens around them.*

When Water feels vulnerable, other defensive qualities surface, including escapism, martyrdom, and holding grudges. Water people use these behaviors to feel emotionally protected and validated. When their deeper needs are unfulfilled, Water becomes defensive.

Defense for Water: Water's dirty laundry
- ⚱ Manipulation
- ⚱ Escapism
- ⚱ Martyrdom
- ⚱ Holding grudges

Our negative qualities are defenses, and defensiveness is where dynamic inner growth (DIG) work comes into play. As a Water-style person, ask yourself, "Am I manipulative?" "Am I moody?" "Am I holding a grudge?" If you answered yes to any of these questions and would like to change that, it's time for Water's DIG. Proceed!

Working It Out: How DIG Work Occurs in Water

PERSONAL DRIVES	BEHAVIOR WHEN VULNERABLE	DIG WORK ABILITIES	BEHAVIOR AFTER DIG WORK
Emotional expression	Moody	Trust	Sensitive
	Clingy	Restraint	Compassionate
Being understood	Manipulative		Affectionate
Protective validation	Escapist		Emotional

DIG begins when you look at your part in a disagreement. For Water style, the questions are, "Was I affectionate or manipulative?" "Did I face a situation head-on or did I run from it?" If you chose to manipulate or escape, you need to look within and recognize what you did. You can do that with trust and restraint, the abilities that enable Water to experience DIG.

Let's check in Bill and Sam again (see dialogue on the following page). This time, Sam is the Water-style person. Bill is getting ready to leave for work, where he has a very important meeting scheduled. Sam is off from work and doesn't want to spend the day alone.

The choice for Sam is to meet his needs by behaving in a manipulative and coercive manner or by showing affection and sensitivity. His willingness to do the DIG work of Water style is what makes the difference. Trust and restraint are the foundation of that work. You need these abilities to change negative expressions into positive ones.

Trust is the ability to know that your partner is not out to get you. It allows you to understand that boundaries and limits are necessary for healthy individuation. Without trust, you might overwhelm someone with emotions. Can you imagine that, Water? Of course you can! With Bill and the missing gift card, he could ask himself, "If my part-

EXTERNAL EXCHANGES WHAT'S HAPPENING	INTERNAL DRAMA WHAT'S REALLY GOING ON
Bill: Okay, I'm out the door. Wish me luck.	He expresses his needs.
Sam: You're leaving already? I thought we had a few more minutes together this morning.	He ignores Bill's request and focuses on his own need for companionship.
Bill: No, I have a big meeting today, and I've got to get out of here now.	He tries to set a boundary.
Sam: Oh, sure, go ahead and just run out the door. 'Bye.	Not only is Sam feeling needy, but he tries to **manipulate** his partner with guilt.
Bill: I'm not running out the door. I need to go.	He restates his boundary.
Sam: Right, right.	He continues to manipulate, mocking Bill and trying to make him feel guilty.
Bill: Honey, you know I'd like nothing more than to stay here with you and have the day off, but this is important! Why don't I call you as soon as I can? I know you're here by yourself today.	Bill restates his truth and, at the same time, gives Sam what he needs. He validates Sam's emotional state. He's not just making trouble for him.
Sam: Aw, thanks. I'm sorry. I'm just missing you already. Here. (He pulls out a sweet good-luck card he has stashed nearby.)	Sam just wanted to feel understood. When he does his DIG work, he can change from negative to positive behavior.
Bill: You're the best!	He loves him for his Water style!

ner doesn't understand all my feelings all the time, does that mean he doesn't love me?" If Bill is honest, he'll know that his behavior was needy and distrustful.

Trust is also about realizing that your "craziness" does not mean you are really crazy. When you trust, you understand that someone can and does accept your emotional nature as normal and as just you being you. Realize that it is possible for someone to misunderstand your emotions and still care about you. As you can see, Water sometimes needs to work with trust.

You also need restraint. This is the ability to slow down, know that too much of a good thing is not a good thing, and contain yourself. Excess, emotional and otherwise, is never the path to Water's happiness. Why not put your amazing emotional expressiveness in perspective and try restraint?

Trust and restraint are the ways that Water digs. Together, they help Water people confront their need for emotional understanding and validation, and realize that things are not always meant to hurt or be achieved through excess.

Own It, Admit It, Be in Touch with It

After working on her DIG, Tinkerbell chooses the best part of Water. She makes the choice to offer protection and compassion. At the point when Captain Hook is about to get rid of Peter Pan for good, Tinkerbell flies in and aids in the rescue.

For Water-style Tinkerbell, empathy and sensitivity prevail as she gives up her wounded feelings and realizes that her love for Peter is more important than her scorn. Through the process of confrontation and self-reflection, Tinkerbell transforms herself. At the risk of her life, she finds Peter, Wendy, and the boys and saves the day. She confronts her negative trait of grudge holding and embraces Water's protectiveness. Tinkerbell shows the dynamic inner growth of Water.

If Water is your style, you can make a choice to look at Water's laundry list and come clean. In the process, emotional neediness can turn into affection and escapism can become imagination. Which type of person would you rather have for a partner?

Water's Time for Introspection

Finding the right time for self-reflection is essential. Water's safe space for DIG work is in activities that enable you to get in touch with your emotions. Of course, you can introspect anytime and anywhere, but when you're doing something that makes you feel emotionally in tune, you will grow from a positive place. By putting yourself in circumstances where you are meeting your own needs, you will create an environment that's free from defensiveness. It is here that you can do your self-reflective DIG work.

Water can have a positive inner growth experience through music, dance, movement, yoga, hiking, time in nature, and visualization. Anything that puts you in touch with your true feelings, one in which you can cry, laugh, or express your mood, is good for self-reflection.

You'll want to look at trust and restraint, and the best way to do that is by turning off your mind and listening to your heart. Try a dance or yoga class. Put yourself in an environment where you can move your body. Body movement creates a vehicle for emotional expression, so it's a great way to elicit your emotional truth. Maybe just put on your headphones, go to a park, and listen to a favorite CD. To get in touch with your feelings, you have to bring them to the surface so that you can take an honest look at them. Music is a fine way to do that. It's an artistic vehicle that helps you travel inside yourself and see how you really feel about someone. Maybe you could differentiate between good feelings for your partner and those that just get in your way.

Maybe you could build a sand castle, dream a little, and give yourself some space to feel that your partner really does love you. Think about how love comes to your life already if you embrace it. You can discover many good things in the safety of Water's activities for introspection.

Water's activities for introspection

- ⚬ Music and art
- ⚬ Dance, movement, and yoga
- ⚬ Nature
- ⚬ Visualization

Water Apologizes

When you apologize, it might occur after a little guilt of your own. Water is very concerned with hurt feelings, and hurting someone else is no better than someone hurting you. Beyond your tears, and perhaps even your copious waterworks, lies the heart of a poet. When "I'm sorry" is in order, it is expressed with art.

Water is particularly intuitive regarding what will touch someone else in just the right way. After all, when you say you're sorry, you want your partner to accept your apology. Well, there's no better way than to speak directly to your lover's soft spot. Music, CDs, DVDs, cards with feeling, poems, and flowers are great ways to ask for forgiveness.

Water expresses an apology with

- ⚬ Original poetry
- ⚬ Music
- ⚬ CDs and DVDs
- ⚬ Cards with feeling

Questions for Self-Awareness

The following questions might lead you to some good discussions with yourself, a friend, or your lover. These are Water's questions for self-reflection and DIG.

I. Could I be more trusting and secure with the love I receive?

2. If I'm emotionally overwhelmed by something, could I appreciate how that might overwhelm my partner as well?
3. Could I let people love me exactly the way they do and not expect a specific demonstration of love?
4. How can I manage worry better?
5. What healthy ways can I retreat into my emotions and feel safe?
6. Does my desire for emotional nurturing make me afraid to give my partner some breathing room?

Water's mantra: I can be objective; I am objective.

Whom Water Needs

To DIG into your stuff, you will need someone who can handle your moodiness and unrealistic attitudes or dreaminess. Most of all, you need someone who can handle your emotional enmeshment and neediness. (Not all the time, obviously.) For you, it would be too emotionally unsafe or isolating if someone didn't understand and care for your feelings.

Your partner is fascinated by your imaginative and sensitive personality. But your partner has to accommodate your manipulative and grudge-holding tactics or your needs will remain unmet. You need to feel emotionally validated and reassured that your feelings are acceptable. If your partner understands these things about you and gives you what you need, the relationship will be a work of art.

DIG Work for Water

The chart on the following page shows how Water outside can be difficult to manage and saturating when expressed in a negative way. The corresponding DIG qualities are shown as well. These are the traits you will want to work on if Water style is your elemental type.

WATER IN NATURE NEGATIVE ATTRIBUTES	YOUR WATERY NATURE DIG WORK QUALITIES
Stagnant	Indolent, idle, escapist, addicted, unrealistic
Cold	Impenetrable, sullen, resentful
Saturating	Hysterical, moody, martyred, frightened
Polluted	Jealous, impenetrable, self-destructive
Dampening	Depressed, defensive
Shallow	Grudge holding, spoiled, immature, time wasting
Murky	Deceptive, sarcastic

12
Earth Works It Out

Earth style is the bottom line. You make it happen, on time and with all the details in order. Earth-style folks want to manifest. That's because the tangible world matters, and you know it! Getting the job done brings value to your life, with the added benefit of stability in your personal life, finances, and reputation.

What Earth needs
* To feel secure
* To be practical
* To have dependability
* To manifest

From chapter 6, you may recall that Earth's positive qualities include being responsible, loyal, and hardworking. These traits establish the basis for Earth's needs. You are the one always offering hard work and loyalty, and you expect nothing less in return.

Your need to feel productive and secure originates from your position as the building one. Earth can bring something to life and get it done with minimal waste. To you, ideas and talking are worthless unless they result in physical manifestations and tangible results. Without you, nothing would come to fruition. Earth finds it unacceptable when things don't get done. Earth is results oriented!

Earth's Choice

Most of the time when Earth-style people try to get what they need, they will act from their positive qualities. But what happens when things get chaotic? What happens when situations arise that cause you to feel ungrounded? That's when you come up against Earth's choice, the decision to act from the positive or negative part of your personality. You choose to create stability and security either through hard work and reliability or greed and rigidity.

In *A Christmas Carol*, Ebenezer Scrooge is consumed with a desire for financial security. Money is his reality. It is everything to him. Scrooge protects himself with his money and runs his life with harsh rigidity. Even on Christmas Eve, he refuses to allow his employee, Bob Cratchit, to go home early. Scrooge is completely mired in his rules, his money, and his rigid structure.

At first, Scrooge is an image of Earth choosing materialism. He is afraid of financial insecurity. He has forgotten that anything exists outside of his bank account and his rigid attitudes toward work and money. Perhaps he doesn't realize that no amount of money or structure can create happiness. So he maintains his security by acting in a rigid, miserly, and stubborn manner. Initially, he gets what he wants—some measure of safety—but misses out on the very people with whom he might share his bounty and find love.

Earth's choice also occurs when you experience physical insecurity and a lack of structure. Somewhere inside, you say, "I don't feel secure with my finances, so I'm going to hoard what I have to get what I need." Often, this happens without your even realizing it. You can remain totally unaware of your motives. You just want to get your needs met. You simply behave in a greedy manner to feel safe. So Earth chooses to act out in a negative way when feeling vulnerable.

Earth and Vulnerability

Earth feels vulnerable when
- 🌱 Feeling uncomfortable or financially insecure
- 🌱 Dealing with impractical things or people
- 🌱 Unable to depend on something or someone
- 🌱 Blocked or unproductive

To show how Earth feels vulnerable, I'd like to explore a simple scene where Earth is inflexible. Sally is our Earth-style person, and Jane is her partner. They are out for dinner, and the check arrives. The external exchanges between Sally and Jane are in the left column. Their internal drama is included on the right.

This example is just one of the many possible conflicts that can result when Earth feels vulnerable. Maybe it started before dinner.

EXTERNAL EXCHANGES WHAT'S HAPPENING	INTERNAL DRAMA WHAT'S REALLY GOING ON
Jane: That was a great dinner.	She had a great time and is ready to enjoy the rest of the evening.
Sally: Yeah, well, it ought to have been. It cost enough!	Rather than focus on the good time, she is distracted by the expense.
Jane: Oh, come on, it was great. Let's pay and get out of here.	She tries to just move on.

Continued on next page

Dr. Craig Martin

Continued from previous page

EXTERNAL EXCHANGES WHAT'S HAPPENING	INTERNAL DRAMA WHAT'S REALLY GOING ON
Sally: Sure. Well, my dinner was less expensive than yours, and I had one drink and you had three, and I didn't have any of the appetizers. So …	She gets **defensive**. By stating the difference between her food and beverage consumption and Jane's, Sally is making strong hints that she only wants to pay for what she ate and drank.
Jane: Right, but why don't we just split it? I'll pick up something else to make up the difference.	She tries to make light of it and move on.
Sally: That's not fair. I don't want to pay for more than my share.	She tries to **defend** herself. But really she's just adhering to behavior that shows her rigidity.
Jane: That's ridiculous. What are we talking about here? A couple of dollars? Are you kidding?	She tries to make some sense out of it.
Sally: Look, you're the one who spends more at dinner. You should pay more.	She **blames** her.
Jane: Spend more? You're the one who wanted to come out for dinner in the first place.	She confronts her, refusing to take the blame.
Sally: So next time, don't say you want to go.	She shows her complete lack of introspection.
Jane: I wish I had done that tonight.	It ends. She's hurt and feeling vulnerable too.

Perhaps Sally was feeling financially insecure when she checked her bank account before they left for dinner. So as the check comes to the table, she is already feeling inflexible and expressing the negative side of Earth. When Jane wants to split the bill, Sally feels vulnerable. That leads her to become defensive.

Earth people could also feel vulnerable if they are physically uncomfortable or if people around them are unreliable. The scenarios are many, but the outcomes are the same: when Earth-style individuals feel vulnerable, they will get defensive. Let's look at how.

Defending Yourself

Scrooge defends his sense of security by acting in a materialistic and stubborn way. Rather than choose the good side of Earth, he tries to maintain structure in his life through greedy, hoarding behavior. This is part of Earth-style defense.

As a defense, Earth-style people retreat to preserve what they have and elevate the practical aspects of life over everything else. In this way, Earth can wall themselves off from emotional concerns and everything that happens around them.

When Earth feels vulnerable, other defensive qualities surface, including stubbornness, withdrawal, and pettiness. These behaviors ensure that Earth feels secure. They represent the negative way Earth attains stability. When their deeper are unfulfilled, Earth people become defensive.

Defense for Earth: Earth's dirty laundry
* Materialistic
* Withdrawn from social interactions
* Petty insistence on details and minutiae
* Inflexible belief system

Our negative qualities are defenses, and defensiveness is where dynamic inner growth (DIG) work comes into play. As an Earth-style person, ask yourself, "Am I overly focused the practical?" "Am I rigid or petty?" "Am I materialistic and miserly?" If you answered yes to any of these and would like to change, it's time for Earth's DIG. Let's go!

Working It Out: How DIG Work Occurs in Earth

PERSONAL DRIVES	BEHAVIOR WHEN VULNERABLE	DIG WORK ABILITIES	BEHAVIOR AFTER DIG WORK
Stability	Rigid	Flexibility	Dependable
Reliability	Petty	Charity	Open-minded
Security	Materialistic		Responsible
	Withdrawn		Productive

DIG begins when you look at your part in a disagreement. For Earth style, the questions are, "Was I reliable or rigid?" "Am I hardworking or materialistic?" If you chose rigid or materialistic, you need to look within and recognize these aspects of yourself. You can do that with flexibility and charity, the abilities that enable Earth to experience DIG.

Let's check in on Sally and Jane again (see dialogue on the following page). This time Jane is the Earth-style person. Jane is waiting for Sally outside a movie theater. Jane had asked her to be there at a specific time, but Sally is running late. She finally arrives.

The choice for Jane is to meet her needs by acting in a rigid and dogmatic manner or by showing flexibility and open-mindedness. Her willingness to do the DIG work of Earth style is what makes the difference. Flexibility and charity are the foundation of that work. You need these abilities to change negative expressions into positive ones.

EXTERNAL EXCHANGES WHAT'S HAPPENING	INTERNAL DRAMA WHAT'S REALLY GOING ON
Sally: Hi. I'm sorry. I got caught in traffic.	She apologizes right away.
Jane: Yeah, great. I asked you to be here ten minutes ago. Now we won't get a good seat.	She's **defensive**. For Jane to feel safe, she needs strict adherence to her rules.
Sally: Okay, well, I'm here now. Let's go in.	She tries to make it better.
Jane: Well, I don't see the point now. I'm not going to get stuck sitting all the way up in the front. I hate that.	She **ups the ante**, making herself more rigid and protective.
Sally: Come on. I think we still have time. Let's try.	She stands in her truth.
Jane: Fine. But if we get in there and don't get a good seat, I'm leaving, and it's your fault.	She **blames** Sally and gets more defensive. Jane feels vulnerable because she thinks her needs won't get met.
Sally: Okay. I understand. Let's see if there's still a good spot. (They go into the theater and, sure enough, they get good seats.) We're in luck. I'll try to be on time next time. Sorry.	She apologizes again and validates Jane's concerns.
Jane: That's okay. These seats are good. Listen, I'll go get popcorn for us! Do you want anything else, sweetie?	She really just wanted to feel secure. When she does her DIG work, she can change from negative to positive behavior.
Sally: No, thanks. You're the best!	She loves her for her Earth style!

Flexibility is the ability to adapt. It allows you to realize that there is more than one way to solve or approach a problem. Flexibility enables you to understand that not everything has to be contained in a specific framework. Without flexibility, your relationship with your partner will suffer severe limitations. Can you imagine that, Earth? Of course you can! With Sally and the dinner check, she could ask herself, "Am I acting a little rigid here?" "Is my behavior petty?" "If we split the check, is someone really taking advantage of me, or am I risking financial inequality?" If Sally were honest, she'd know she was behaving as a stickler and in a rigid way regarding correctness.

Flexibility is also about realizing that you can't expect everyone to conform to your set of rules. When you loosen up a little, you understand that it's okay to enjoy dessert before dinner every now and then. You may find it helpful to trace the origin of your set of rules. As you can see, Earth sometimes needs to work with flexibility.

You also need charity, which is the ability to give to others. Charity teaches you that the more you give, the more you receive, and you can find happiness by helping others. Why not put that amazing sense of order and material savvy to good use and try charity?

Flexibility and charity are the ways that Earth digs. Together, they help Earth individuals confront their need for financial security and physical comfort. Flexibility and charity also help Earth realize that there's more than one answer in a situation and that it is safe to share.

Own It, Admit It, Be in Touch with It

After working on his DIG, Scrooge chooses the best part of Earth. He makes the choice to offer charity and generosity. After a long night of introspection at the hands of the Christmas ghosts, Scrooge sees the light and decides to mend his ways. He wakes on Christmas morning to the joyful realization that he can give of himself and receive a different kind of reward—that of affection and community.

For Earth-style Scrooge, responsibility and dependability prevail as he gives up his greed and restrictions and realizes that his generosity toward the Cratchit family is more important than his miserly and protective attitude. Through the process of confrontation and self-reflection, he transforms himself. Stepping outside his greed, Scrooge wakes from his unconsciousness and saves the day. He rejects his greedy nature and chooses his positive, generous side. Scrooge shows the DIG of Earth.

If Earth is your style, you can make a choice to look at Earth's laundry list and come clean. In the process, restrictions can turn into productivity and rigidity can become responsibility. Which type of person would you rather have for a partner?

Earth's Time for Introspection

Finding the right time for self-reflection is key. Earth's safe space for DIG work is in hands-on activities or those that allow you to create order. As you build or organize, you can reflect on your need for dependability and security. Of course, you can introspect anytime and anywhere, but when you feel productive, you will grow from a positive place. By putting yourself in circumstances where you meet your own needs, you create an environment that's free from defensiveness. It is here that you can do your self-reflective DIG work.

Earth-style people can have a positive inner growth experience through gardening, exercise, repair work, building something, cooking, cleaning, and organizing. Any activity where you can see your efforts turn into practical results, create order, or develop a purposeful routine is good for self-reflection.

You'll want to look at flexibility and charity, and the best way to do that is by bringing order to a disorganized situation. Try gardening or building something useful. Put yourself in an environment where you can follow instructions and create an effective end product. Exercise is a great place for Earth-style people to get in touch with their bodies and do some thinking. How about repairing something around the house? Hands-on projects are good ways for you to take an honest look at your behaviors and actions. As you clean the house, you'll consider how generosity can make you feel more secure.

Maybe you could build that rose garden, cook that special dinner, and give yourself space to see that giving is better than receiving. You can discover many good things in the safety of Earth's activities for introspection.

Earth's activities for introspection

- ❦ Exercise
- ❦ Gardening
- ❦ Repair work and organizing
- ❦ Cooking, cleaning, housework/yard work

Earth Apologizes

When you apologize, your partner can expect some tangible payoff. Earth sees "I'm sorry" as a need for servitude, or at least a fine dinner out. So beyond pulling out your checkbook and making it all better, you could do some chore you've been saying you'll get around to. Perhaps acting helpful or giving a back rub might represent the perfect way for you to apologize.

Because Earth is grounded, practical and reliable forms of apology are perfect for you. You could agree to do your partner's chores for a couple of days. Give a little gift that might make your significant other's life easier or more enjoyable. That's a great way for you to ask for forgiveness.

Earth expresses an apology with

- ❦ Gift giving
- ❦ Doing unexpected chores
- ❦ Helpfulness
- ❦ Giving back/foot rubs or doting in some way

Questions for Self-Awareness

The following questions might lead you to some good discussions with yourself, a friend, or your lover. These are Earth's questions for self-reflection and DIG.

1. Could I be more willing to bend my rules under certain circumstances?
2. How would it feel if I didn't care so much about how things looked?
3. When was the last time I made a mess on purpose?
4. What excites me?
5. Are there things that could help me cut loose?
6. Does my desire for stability make me afraid to speak up and voice my real needs or concerns?

Earth's mantra: I can roll with it; I roll with it.

Whom Earth Needs

To DIG into your stuff, you will need someone who can handle your stubborn and appearance-oriented nature. Most of all, you will need someone who accepts your organized and regimented behavior. (Not all the time, obviously.) But for you, it would be too chaotic or frustrating if you didn't have reliability in your relationship.

Your partner might admire your sense of responsibility and the amazing way you get the job done. But your partner has to accommodate your routine and orderly life or your needs will not be met. You need to feel secure in the relationship, and you love your partner's dependability. If your partner understands these things about you and gives you what you need, the relationship will be an abundant one.

DIG Work for Earth

The chart below shows how Earth outside can be difficult to manage and unproductive when expressed in a negative way. The corresponding DIG qualities are shown as well. These are the traits you will want to work on if Earth style is your elemental type.

EARTH IN NATURE NEGATIVE ATTRIBUTES	YOUR EARTHY NATURE DIG WORK QUALITIES
Unfruitful	Wasteful, careless
Unstable	Limited, dull, dense, possessive, fussy
Muddy	Extravagant, excessive, irresponsible
Hollow	Materialistic, petty, greedy, timid
Dry	Dogmatic, inflexible, stubborn, obstinate, reserved, unyielding, limiting, regimented, dogmatic, stagnant

Part III

Elemental Combinations

13
In the Mix

We learned in part 2 that healthy relationships are the result of true intimacy and dynamic inner growth (DIG). These chapters demonstrated ways to achieve intimacy by meeting your deeper needs, confronting your negative qualities, and interacting with your partner in a positive, loving manner. We saw that each element has its own DIG work to do, and that by looking at ourselves more honestly we can work out our differences.

Now it's time to mix things up! Let's find out what to expect when elements combine with one another. Keep in mind that no elemental combination is better than others. Any two people could work if you are willing to work the mix. So do not expect to find that a particular elemental combination is a deal breaker. That's not the way that intimacy works. When you are willing and able to meet your partner's deeper needs, and they yours, then you will find a lasting match.

This section of the book will help you gain a general understanding of various elemental combinations. After learning how your deeper needs interact with those of another elemental type, you'll take a look at what comes easily and what presents challenges in the relationship. Remember to take your time, be flexible, and allow yourself to experience the creativity and fun of being with someone who has differences from you. Those differences should be exciting and enjoyable. Explore them and allow yourself to grow in the discovery.

Not every couple will encounter the same issues. For example, one Earth/Fire combination might disagree about how to spend money, while another Earth/Fire combination could see eye-to-eye about finances, but have problems with balancing home and work. An individual brings his or her life history, personality, preferences, aversions, and fears to interactions with others, and this background can affect what gets the most emphasis in a relationship. Two Air-style men both have a deeper need for freedom and personal space, but may express that need differently. One might want to have personal time to hang out with his guy friends, while the other might want uninterrupted time to simply read books in his favorite chair. Both men need time for their own thing, but each in their own way. Seeing your partner's needs and then meeting those needs is a great gesture of love.

You discovered your elemental type after completing the questionnaire in chapter 2. When it's time to find out someone else's elemental type, you can do so in several ways. If it's a recent connection, you could slip some of the questions into a conversation. If it's someone you've known for a while or feel comfortable with, you could give that person a photocopy of the quiz or have fun asking him or her the questions. You may even know someone so well that his or her elemental style is fairly obvious to you! Enjoy the process as you discover more about yourself and other people.

In the next chapters, you'll learn what happens when your elemental style combines with other elemental styles. Each combination has its own positive aspects and challenges. For each combination, I make a suggestion that could create harmony for that couple, but it is just one suggestion. As you get to know your relationship better, you will have your own ideas for bringing you closer together. Try those ideas! They are the result of working it out and you deserve the closeness. Knowing what to anticipate when you mix your style with another will help you navigate the rocky patches, clear the path, and more fully enjoy the journey.

Ready to learn more about how your element mixes with others? Good, because now you're really in for the ride!

14
Fire in the Mix

FIRE + FIRE = Fireworks

Snapshot: All that glitters

Highlights: Active, passionate, creative

Must-haves: Since you're both Fire types, you and your partner have the same deeper needs in a relationship. Each wants to feel important and have the other recognize how great you are. Make sure you find ways to express your love and communicate how much you respect and admire each other. For this relationship to work, you need to develop a mutual admiration society.

The Pluses: You stimulate each other's passion for living, making Fire/Fire a terrific matchup. This relationship is fun! There is so much drive between you that boredom while watching the grass grow is not going to be an issue. You are always on the go, doing interesting, exciting things. There's never a dull moment when the two of you are together.

What comes easily in this relationship is the way you spark each other's creativity. If you're planning a weekend away, one of you might suggest Mexico while the other talks about climbing the Mayan pyramids of Teotihuacán at the same time. Couples of the same element are in sync, and for Fire/Fire that connection is the thrill of enjoying, exploring, and savoring the world around you.

Together, you produce a formidable team. A Fire/Fire partnership is a force to be reckoned with. Each of you can count on the other to guard your back, and you both have the creative enormity to find solutions to the most difficult dilemmas. You are superheroes in your own adventure, making each day together a wide-eyed and enthusiastic joyride.

The Minuses: When you start to feel competitive with each other, take a serious look at what's going on in the relationship. Competition can crop up when one of you feels unappreciated, doesn't have personal space to shine, feels ignored, or isn't getting enough attention. Whatever the cause, competition can leave you feeling scorched.

When either of you feels unappreciated, an argument isn't far behind. Fire can initiate some of the biggest blowups since the Big Bang. You see, you love drama, so you're not afraid of exploding when you're upset. When anger erupts, you can rage like a wildfire, even in public.

In a fight, you will go to any lengths to make your point, get your way, and prove your importance. In the process, you could destroy your relationship or at least inflict major damage. Look before you leap into the abyss of anger.

The Challenge: Make sure each of you has an area where you can take the spotlight and gain special attention. One of you might consider the kitchen a personal domain, while the other takes charge of interior decorating or vacation planning. Work toward giving each other space to express and excel. That way you can both have a place to shine and be the focal point of praise and adoration. Can you praise and adore your partner? Start with lots of compliments. They go a long way for the Fire/Fire couple.

Suggestion: Plan, design, or create something together. Sit on the floor at the bookstore, maybe in front of the travel, cooking, or interior design sections. Share your ideas with each other. Dream big, and watch your combined vision emerge.

In Private: The healthy Fire/Fire couple is all over each other just about all the time. Your sexual attraction is off the charts. On your own, you're hot, and together, you're even hotter. The Fire/Fire couple can count on a fun, active sex life, with an original performance each time. Creativity and passion come together for some full-scale bedroom pyrotechnics. So be careful you don't burn the bed, or the floor for that matter.

In Public: Wherever you go, you two are a big presence. As a couple, people are drawn to your warmth and larger-than-life personalities. You just fit together. You feel right, look right, and generate excitement. You're the "it" couple of your crowd, the one with the fun ideas, exciting stories, and dramatic adventures. Being in the know makes you the couple everyone wants to know.

Some Fire/Fire Advice

Dear Dr. Craig,

My fiancée and I have been living together for the past year. I just graduated from law school, and she's finishing up her degree in fashion design. We're going to get married after she gets out of school. Last night, my fiancée showed me drawings of her wedding dress and then got annoyed because she thought I wasn't paying attention. She slammed down her drawing pad and stormed out of the room. I've looked at those drawings a hundred times. I don't understand her fixation with the dress. I mean, we haven't even set a wedding date. I'm madly in love with my fiancée and know she's the one for me. But how do I get her to understand that I've seen enough of that dress for the time being?

—BURNED OUT

Dear Burned,

Sounds to me like your fiancée needs some attention and praise. I'm figuring that you're both Fire types. You each need to shine in your chosen careers and at home with each other. I understand how you feel: you think you've done enough already. But I also see how your fiancée could get upset. She needs more recognition for the wedding dress she's designed. If you want your fiancée for keeps, you'd better find time to acknowledge how wonderful she is and meet her needs. And how about that wedding date? Could it be that her showing you the dress a hundred times is just a big hint that you're not getting? Set a date and watch things cool down for you.

—DR. CRAIG

FIRE + AIR = Blast off!

Snapshot: A hot-air balloon

Highlights: Enthusiastic, intellectual, articulate

Must-haves: In this relationship, Fire needs recognition and praise, a sense of importance, and space to create. Air needs to feel unrestricted, engage in social interactions, and keep things light and humorous. For the relationship to work, Air needs to fan the flames of Fire's creativity with lots of attention and compliments. And Fire needs to keep Air's interest by remaining flexible, informative, and fun.

The Pluses: Together, you make a great creative team. Fire generates ideas, and Air gives the ideas verbal expression. You really get off on collaborating with each other. It's fun and exciting to brainstorm and watch the ideas grow into even bigger ideas.

For each of you, the intellectual and creative part of your relationship is a very big turn-on. What comes easily to you is enthusiasm. The two of you are excited about spending time together, talking with each other, and inspiring thoughts. What might end up as just a passing notion gets articulated into a successful venture or innovative concept.

There is never a dull moment for the Fire/Air combo. How could there be? You always have something to discuss, and you're always developing new ideas, and you're excited about possibilities that await you on your next adventure.

The Minuses: Watch out for exhaustion. Air breathes life into Fire, but the two can get used up in the process. At the start, you need to experience each other in small doses. Too much exposure too soon can leave you both feeling depleted. Better to take it slow and get used to each other's energy.

Fire needs space to shine and Air needs space to feel free. If Fire feels unappreciated or Air feels boxed in, an argument is inevitable. When Fire gets angry, it would be wise to watch out for an incinerating flamethrower. When Air gets angry, he or she can blow cold. Air may famously say "Whatever," dismissing Fire's anger or hurt feelings. This will enrage Fire and lead to an even bigger argument.

Sometimes Fire will get angry just to get attention from Air, who at times can appear distant, distracted, and far away. When Air needs space, Fire could interpret that as being neglected. That won't play well in the long run, and you'll need to address it before things get really chilly.

The Challenge: The biggest risk in this relationship is too much exposure to each other too soon. If Fire gets too big a blast of Air, he or she feels overblown and overheated. If Air gets too much Fire, he or she can feel used up. This could easily make Air act in a dismissive and unfocused way. When the focus is not on Fire, you know what happens! Can you recognize that Air needs room for their freedom-loving exploits but that you're still their number one? Just because Air has many interests doesn't mean they're not interested in you!

Suggestion: Spend time together but go about your own business. Return to each other with your individual perspectives. This could be as simple as reading the same book and then discussing it. Or perhaps go to a museum together, move about it at your own speed, and then meet for lunch in the museum café. Revisit the two pieces of art that you both loved the most and tell each other why!

In Private: Sex for the Fire/Air couple is versatile and often verbal. Fire and Air both love to assume roles and act out scenarios. When you playact, Fire gets the starring role, but Air is the writer/director. Make the most of your creative talents. New locations and wide-ranging options are best for you. Use the phone or send that sexy text message. You both aren't shy about making your needs known. The best part of the bedroom is when it feels new, raw, and exciting every time.

In Public: Fire and Air make a terrific pair. You have fascinating conversations, get excited about each other's successes, and keep the energy so high that you both stay interesting. As storytellers, there are no better, and together, you make people laugh. Other couples enjoy being around you because you're stimulating and communicative and know how to make things happen. You set trends, and people love that about you.

Some Fire/Air Advice

Dear Dr. Craig,

I love my work as an architect because it allows me to express myself creatively. I not only design houses, but I also work out of my house. That's the problem right now. Ever since I started working at home, my wife thinks she can barge into my office anytime and start talking, usually about nothing important. Other noise pollution includes her blasting the television and radio and talking loudly on the phone. During working hours, the only time I get anything done is when my wife is at her part-time job. Don't get me wrong. I'm crazy about my wife. She is the funniest, wittiest, most interesting person I know, and we make a great team. I just need her to understand that I have to focus on my work without distractions. What can I do?

—WIT'S END

Dear Wit's,

You sound like a Fire type who gets a lot of recognition from your work. I'd guess, then, that you might not need so much attention at home. That's okay for you, but what about your chatty Air-type wife? You might consider something unimportant, but she might think it's a big deal. And she needs to share it with you. Above all, Air types want communication, and you are the sounding board of her heart. You need a Do Not Disturb sign on your office door, and she needs to respect it. After work, you should set aside some time for her. While you're making your mark in the world, you need to remember how she made her mark on you. Earplugs and noise reduction devices are also recommended.

—DR. CRAIG

FIRE + WATER = Alchemy

Snapshot: Steamy heat

Highlights: Creative, emotional, deep

Must-haves: While this relationship presents challenges, it can work and even thrive if you keep in mind each other's deeper needs. Fire needs to feel important, get recognition and praise, and have space in the relationship to create. Water needs emotional validation, reassurance, and protection. To keep the relationship healthy, Fire has to allow time and space for Water's emotional responses and Water has to keep Fire stoked with sincere appreciation.

The Pluses: Fire and Water can have a profound effect on each other. Fire becomes more sensitive when exposed to Water's emotional depth, and Water becomes more expressive when connected to Fire's creative passion. The Fire/Water mix produces steam, an altogether new and powerful force.

Transformation is possible as Fire becomes more in touch with his or her emotions and more aware of other people's needs, while Water becomes more aware of the world beyond his or her feelings and realizes the excitement that's possible when connected with a creative force.

The experience for the Fire/Water pair is a modification of the two individual characters when they are together as a couple. While this is not easy, Fire can burn off emotional stagnation for Water and Water can cool and focus Fire into a useful and powerful creative light.

The Minuses: It's going to be difficult for the Fire/Water couple to meet each other's deeper needs. It is not impossible, but there is a real fundamental difference in their approach to life. This can cause Fire's flame to feel dimmed and Water's feelings to feel singed. You may begin to feel as if you're neutralizing each other. When this happens, you can end up feeling less like yourselves and more like an overheated or watered-down version of who you really are.

Fire can experience Water's emotional reactions as excessive neediness and feel dampened and let down. If Water experiences Fire's extroverted behavior as course and abrasive, it will retreat and may become melancholy.

Either abrasive behavior or emotional neediness are certain to lead to a fight. When this happens, Fire and Water seem like strangers to each other. Without even a basic understanding of what makes each other tick, they quickly lose tolerance for one another. Fire starts hearing Water's emotional expressions as whining, and Water experiences Fire's high energy as arrogance.

Watch out if Fire ignores Water's sensitivity and emotional needs. Water craves understanding, and if you, as a Fire, are too preoccupied with big ideas to pay attention, Water will become an emotional wreck.

The Challenge: The key here is awareness. Fire and Water have vastly different needs. Keeping that in mind will ensure greater success. Water has to back off when it overwhelms Fire with emotional demands. Fire has to develop an appreciation for Water's emotional responses. Can you accept each other in a way that allows your partner to be different? You love each other for those differences, so why not make a steam engine rather than get scalded.

Suggestion: Pick an activity that you both like. Go bowling, skiing, rock climbing, or play mini-golf. It's time to bring out the inner kid in both of you. Be playful, have fun, let your creativity and imagination guide you to laughter and fond memories.

In Private: Fire and Water can enjoy a deep, fulfilling sex life. That steam engine comes to mind again. All the passion of Fire combined with the emotional complexity of Water turns creative lovemaking into a hot tub of delights. Fire is unequaled at romantic gestures, and Water soaks them in. This gives Fire the opportunity to see the effect their creative juices have on a tender and sensitive heart.

In Public: The Fire/Water couple is an expressive and imaginative pair. When you recount stories about an exotic vacation or even a trip to the art museum, people feel like they've been to the movies. Fire tells the dramatic parts and Water recounts the deeper nuance. Together, you paint a compelling, meaningful picture of whatever you've experienced. Others like being around you because excitement takes on a rich, full longevity. All your effort pays off as you create a lasting impact!

Some Fire/Water Advice

Dear Dr. Craig,

I've been dating my boyfriend for a few months and have never felt so emotionally connected to anybody. We don't even need to talk but can just sense what the other feels. On top of this, he's a talented artist and so imaginative. I'm nuts about this guy, except for one thing: he complains a lot. He yammers on and on about his mother, his friends, and his job. I work all day, go to law school at night, and study every spare chance I get. My boyfriend gets so whiny and repetitious sometimes with his grievances that sometimes I feel like all I want to do is make a closing argument. What can I do?

—*PITY PARTY NO MORE*

Dear Pity,

Your boyfriend is a Water type and needs lots of reassurance. While he's busy venting his emotional frustrations, you're trying to get ready for your day at the bench. As a Fire type, there are limits to how much nurturing and mushy stuff you can offer. After all, you don't want all that Water to put you out. Helping him resolve his emotional drama is not really your responsibility. But you can listen. That's what he needs. And I'm sure that most of the time your optimistic and persuasive manner brings him back to the bright side. Suggest that he apply his aggravations to his art and see how imaginative he can really be!

—DR. CRAIG

FIRE + EARTH = Hot property

Snapshot: A beautifully wrapped gift

Highlights: Enthusiastic, dependable, productive

Must-haves: A good relationship rarely just happens, and that's the case here. Fire and Earth have to invest the time and effort it takes to understand each other. Fire needs Earth to offer appreciation, and

Earth needs Fire to offer reliability. When Fire keeps its word and Earth gives a good word, these two make a great pair.

The Pluses: Fire has the ideas and Earth is like a kiln that brings the ideas to life. While Fire may burst with concepts, Earth is the one that knows how to take those concepts and make them work. This can be a truly satisfying match.

Fire inspires Earth, and Earth brings abstract ideas to material form. Together, you manifest—bringing tangible results to fruition. When Fire says, "Let's put up shelves in the living room," Earth makes it happen with contentment and an added Earthy practical creativity.

What comes easily in this relationship is a sense of purpose. Together, you get things done and feel good about what you've accomplished. That new bookshelf in the living room didn't stay in the design phase very long. Together, you create, plan, and execute so that you can move on to the next accomplishment.

Abounding with ideas and adventure, Fire makes Earth's life more exciting, while Earth brings Fire down to earth and makes his or her ideas more practical. A Fire/Earth couple brings about concrete changes in their lives and in the lives of those around them. When you really embrace Earth's grounding, Fire, you can move mountains.

The Minuses: One of the big challenges in this relationship is a difference in your travel speeds. Fire likes to move quickly, and Earth wants to move more slowly. Between "hurry up" and "slow down" there is the possibility of a lot of frustration.

If Fire tries to rush Earth, Earth gets overwhelmed and aggravated. When Fire has to slow down, he or she can feel confined and angry. Fire likes to have their way and have it now. This doesn't always work so well with someone who can dig their heels in and not budge.

Even small annoyances may set off disagreements or lead to hurt feelings. Fire could burst in with a new idea and have to wait until

Earth finishes reading a newspaper story before getting a response. While this can leave Fire to stew in his or her own impatience, they need to realize that Earth must finish one thing before starting something else.

It is possible that Earth becomes infuriating to Fire. Earth may seem so unmoved by your grand displays of insistence and forthright demands. They may try to give Fire the silent treatment, and that's one thing you will not stand for. Hurtful accusations can flair, and that's not going to ever make things work out well.

The Challenge: Understand that there must be a speed that works for the both of you. Without blaming each other for the speed, you're comfortable with traveling at different speeds when necessary. Perhaps you even allow each other to do so. You may find that you'll end up at the destination together anyway. You can't force each other to be something you're not. So can you meet each other when all is said and done? Maybe then the blaze of creativity and the steadiness of substance will have made something of real beauty.

Suggestion: Plan a little dinner for a couple of friends that you both know. Take your time to plan the menu together, the beverages, the music, and the dessert! Do the prep work as a couple. Divide up the chores. Then when your guests arrive, put it all together with enthusiasm and proficiency. Have a WOW moment with each other when they leave.

In Private: Fire loves to arouse and stimulate, which works out well because Earth types are sensual with a capital *S*. The Fire/Earth motto is "If you can't stand the heat, get out of the bedroom." This pair is like an oven. With Earth as the enduring and steadfast lover, Fire has a consistent place to play out his or her ideas. When Fire is in charge and Earth lets go, you can both discover passion and adoration.

In Public: As a couple, you'll probably have good social standing. Earth knows how to pursue success, while Fire knows how to bring excitement into any gathering. People respect and admire your status and good reputation and want you on their boards and advisory groups. This gives you many friends and colleagues who are attracted to your multifaceted capabilities. Your wide range of interests, from decorating to hiking, fits in well with lots of different folks. Fire might even convince Earth to get on a roller coaster for a group jaunt to the amusement park, especially if it doesn't go too fast.

Some Fire/Earth Advice

Dear Dr. Craig,

The other day I was out with the guy I'm dating when we ran into a street fair. It looked awesome, with lots of artwork and a live band, and I was excited about checking it out. We were headed to dinner at a nearby restaurant, however, and my date didn't want to be late. I was really upset. I'm all for punctuality, but I need spontaneity too! Where was his sense of adventure? Anyway, I insisted that we go, but he was unhappy about it. I haven't talked to him since that night. I really like him, but don't know how to deal with his one-track mind.

—FEELING UNFAIR

Dear Unfair,

Why miss out on an opportunity, right? Well, for your Earth-type boyfriend, the opportunity was already planned. He sees the street fair as a distraction, not an adventure. You are a spontaneous Fire type, and your need for excitement over-rides a set routine. For you, the restaurant will be there next week, but the street fair is now. For him, the restaurant is now, and it probably has been since breakfast. Earth types need a set plan, and going off that plan is very disruptive. It is possible, though, for you to plan something spontaneous. Why not suggest going downtown and doing whatever comes up? Let the moment guide you. Explore. See if you can put him on the one track of discovery!

—DR. CRAIG

THE GETAWAY

Different couples respond to the same experience in different ways. Fire loves to travel and go off on fun getaways. What happens when Fire pairs up with others? Let's take a look.

Fire/Fire Couple: This getaway is about excitement. The Fire/Fire couple will make big plans and try to cram as much activity as possible into the visit. The two of you can hit the beach, the Everglades, and the alligator farm, and manage to go deep-sea fishing and scuba diving all in a weekend. The trip will be a hit as long as each of you gets a chance to do something special.

Fire/Air Couple: This getaway is about exploration. Fire has the ideas and Air has the information. Florida? Air just devoured a novel by Carl Hiaasen and read a *New Yorker* article about coral conservation. Once in the Sunshine State, Fire and Air find plenty to do together and don't mind doing some things alone. Fire might want to go snorkeling for an hour while Air explores a local museum. You're good traveling companions and sure to have a great time away from home.

Fire/Water Couple: This getaway is about romance. During your trip to Florida, Water will get excited about strolls on the beach and candlelit dinners, not to mention emotional lovemaking and breakfast in bed. Fire gets excited about these things too, but also loves the change of scenery because it sparks lots of new ideas. You'll have a wonderful time as long as Fire showers the bed with rose petals and Water understands that Fire needs time for something daring, such as waterskiing or an amateur drive in Daytona.

Fire/Earth Couple: This getaway is about proactive relaxation. Earth loves ease and comfort and enjoys chilling out by the pool. Perhaps there's poolside bingo with a dinner for two as the prize. Fire loves a chance to win! Later, how about a full spa treatment at the hotel? You're both up for that. Fire can be treated royally and Earth can be pampered. What a match. So while Earth isn't dying to visit the alligator farm, he or she will do it, if Fire agrees to kick back later.

15
Air in the Mix

AIR + AIR = Breathing room

Snapshot: Free spirits

Highlights: Curious, intellectual, independent

Must-haves: Two Air types have the same deeper needs in a relationship. Each wants to feel unrestricted and mentally stimulated. There is plenty of agreement on social interactions and in keeping things light and humorous. To make this relationship work, give each other lots of space, but make sure you spend quality time together.

The Pluses: Air people really get each other. What others might call flakiness Air understands as the need for flexibility and freedom. With another Air, you don't have to explain why you need space or justify why you need to spend time with friends. You are on the same wavelength, and that sounds good.

Since you both have wide-ranging interests and stay on top of current events and popular culture, the two of you have plenty to discuss. There is always something of interest to banter about. Both the newspaper in bed on Sundays and the local community organization are good for you.

You really get each other's sense of humor and laugh a lot when you're together. This makes going to the movies or theater quite the spectacle, with the two of you laughing yourselves into a tizzy. Yet no matter how connected you are in the moment, you will allow each other the independent time to do your own thing. The Air/Air couple lives without attachment, guilt, or any other emotional baggage.

This makes staying out of each other's way easy. Without possessiveness there arises a joy in having found another freedom-loving soul. Fear of being bound or restricted is removed from your partnership, and a true friendship of lovers emerges as your path.

The Minuses: While you're good at giving each other space, you can run into trouble if you give each other too much room. Excessive time apart can result in a sterile, superficial connection. The distance, which develops from too much "on your own" time, won't leave you with much to talk about.

Ironic, isn't it, how two talkative people can just run out of words? Your relationship could grow unfeeling and wordless. Without all the chitchat and humor, an Air couple is going to have a hard time finding common ground.

Air types are notorious for being able to shut down and detach from others. If this happens in a relationship between two Airs—wow—it can grow mighty cold in the space between. Even if you're in the same room, you may not even recognize that the other is there. Quite the argument style!

If your connection turns sterile, one or both of you may decide to move on to more stimulating territory. Air needs a constant flow of new tidbits of information and knowledge. If you're not going to get that from each other, then there is little use in staying together. Your time together will only become forced, and Air can hardly be forced into anything.

The Challenge: If you want a romantic partnership to last, watch for signs that you're giving each other too much space and have grown distant. Keep your connection strong and you'll never be bored around each other. By making dates with one another, putting each other on the calendar, and setting aside time to socialize together, you can keep each other connected to the cloud nine of your love. What do you think it will take to prevent your relationship from turning shallow or distant? Don't forget the Sunday morning paper-in-bed routine! It's you!

Suggestion: Besides reading the Sunday paper in bed next to each other, do the crossword puzzle. Start listening to audio books when you're in the car together. Intellectual stimulation is vital. If you've met a new couple on one of your journeys here and there, invite them out for dinner. Talk and listen, and then go over the experience together. Your opinions really matter to each other.

In Private: It is said that the most important sex organ in the body is the brain, and Air would agree. The right word and even a joke will do more to turn on Air than champagne and candlelight. Humor is provocative, and you know how to turn a laugh into the giggles of romantic bliss. And while you spend much of the day hiding behind those reading glasses, you have no trouble letting your hair down in bed. From the whisper of sweet nothings to the verbal outcries of ecstasy, Air/Air love is never a silent feature.

In Public: Everyone wants to spend time with the world's easiest couple. Not only are you intelligent and funny, but your trouble-free natures make planning with you a delight as well. Other people find an Air/Air match engaging, informative, and hilarious. Between the two of you, a whole evening could be filled with one interesting story after another. There are so many to tell and such funny twists to deliver. Keeping people on their toes is a trademark of you as a duo. Whether laughing or fielding your many questions, people use their minds when you're around, and they love it!

Some Air/Air Advice

Dear Dr. Craig,

I've been with my husband for over five years. We talk, we socialize, and we love to read and do crosswords together. At least we do when we see each other. We're both so busy that we barely have time for each other anymore. Seems like we both have so much of our own going on that sometimes I wonder if our marriage has turned into just a series of text messages. When we got married, we agreed that freedom was important for us. I wonder if we've taken that a bit too far. It's time to do something about it, but I just don't know what.

—BUSY WITHOUT HIM

Dear Busy,

A little time invested in your relationship can put you both back in touch. You sound like two Air types, and it's easy for freedom lovers to become distant. Lots of space and a full schedule are great for your personal goals, but maybe not so good for a strong bond. You need to reconnect. You mentioned things that you like to do together. It's time to do more of those. A conversation about all this, a good laugh, and some renewed experiences together will get you back in sync. Have a dinner party! Rent a comedy! Talk to each other! You love all this about each other.

—DR. CRAIG

AIR + FIRE = Soaring intensity

Snapshot: Riding in a convertible

Highlights: Smart, passionate, enthusiastic

Must-haves: While you complement each other, Air and Fire have different deeper needs. Above all, Air needs to feel free and have lots of space for personal interests, friends, and social engagements. Fire can give Air space as long as Air offers lots of attention, admiration, and compliments. The language skills of Air will come in mighty handy when Fire's need for praise kicks in. Air/Fire is a great fit because Air can let Fire have the spotlight and Fire can let Air do his or her own thing.

The Pluses: Combined, Air and Fire generate a lot of heat, in every way imaginable. Air loves to discuss, and Fire is an exciting conversational partner. Enthusiasm and a real childlike sense of wonder make Fire an enticing source of knowledge for Air. Anyone who is so charged up must have something important to offer. At least that's the way that Air sees it, and more often than not, it's true.

Fire bursts with ideas and loves the way Air articulates them and gives them breadth. There is always something to add when Air is in the conversation, and Fire finds that fascinating. The Air/Fire couple makes a particularly amazing brainstorming team. They bounce ideas off each other with an unrivaled speed and generate new thoughts that are novel, humorous, and clever.

Spontaneity comes naturally to both of you, so you're ready at a moment's notice for the next event or adventure. Air is never bored with the same old same old when Fire is at hand, while Fire finds a true, interactive lover and an Air partnership where competition is lessened and action is high on the agenda.

The Minuses: This relationship burns red-hot, which is great, until it's not. The Air/Fire combination can move at really fast speeds, and this may lead to burnout. An enthusiastic communication can turn into a heated argument in a flash. Too much too fast, and then you crash and burn. The problem is that Air may not be able to focus on specifics for the same period of time that Fire can. First you are talking together, then the talking becomes too intense, and suddenly Air glazes over. If Fire is all worked up in expressing him- or herself, they may not want to change gears so quickly, and an argument begins.

Air needs time to wander and change the channel fairly often. This need for shifting focus doesn't go over so well with a Fire partner. Fire should pretty much always be the focus, so Air's divided attention is not going to play out very well when Fire feels ignored.

Arguments between Air and Fire are often a chicken/egg scenario. Which came first? Did Air ignore Fire, or did Fire make Air feel restricted? Whatever the cause, Air and Fire express their anger in different ways. Air tries to get away, and Fire demands attention. This makes for a tough discrepancy between "leave me alone" and "let's fix this now!"

The Challenge: To prevent crashing and burning, take each other in small doses, especially if the relationship is new. The Air/Fire combination is just too powerful for full-scale exposure even after you've grown accustomed to each other's energy. To stop an argument in progress, forget the blame game and communicate. What can you do if you feel overwhelmed by the high energy? How can you cool down?

Room for private time, in unison with moments of intense adoration, will go a long way between you.

Suggestion: Surely on your bookshelf there is a poetry book or two. Or perhaps you might find a mystery or tragic romance or a much-loved novel from the past. Each of you go to your books and pick one at random. Open to wherever your fingers find and read to each other. Giggles, laughter, and all-out freaky coincidences are permitted.

In Private: Air didn't know how passionate love could be until Fire arrived on the scene. While Fire loves a quickie, there's more to romance than a roll in the hay. Fire has quite a big range when it comes to creative lovemaking. So if action is what you want, then your superhero has arrived. Able to handle all the variety and energy of really wild sex, the Air/Fire couple is not exactly shy. In fact, your neighbors definitely have the windows closed!

In Public: You are a couple that gets noticed. There's laughter and style shining off you, and people can't help but want a little bit of your action. Others see you as informed and charged up. You know the places to go, and you show up there. There's excitement between you that's palpable. The energy that you exchange is so high-voltage that strangers even come up to see what's going on. That couple in the crowd that looks so good, laughs out loud, and presents a unified force together is probably an Air/Fire match.

Some Air/Fire Advice

Dear Dr. Craig,

The woman I'm dating is great! She's vivacious and a whole lot of fun! Trouble is, I feel like I can never win with her. It isn't only when we have an argument; it happens even when I'm just being funny. Like the other day, I was telling her that I had opened a can of soda at work and it had almost sprayed all over me. I thought this was funny. But she needed to point out I could have gotten my work clothes dirty, and since I was picking her up straight from work, that really wouldn't have been so great. What do I have to do to catch a break around here?

—FIZZLED OUT

Dear Fizzled,

Sounds to me like you've got a real Fire type on your hands, and Fire types can be quite preoccupied with themselves. You can win but just need to know how to pick your battles. Fire types love flattery. Maybe if you'd ended by saying, "I'm so glad I didn't get any soda on my clothes because I was meeting you," she would have laughed because you'd acknowledged her concerns. As an Air type, you think quickly on your feet, so try to stay one step ahead. She only wants to know you're thinking of her and treating her as a priority. And keeping an extra set of clothes with you at work might be a good idea too!

—DR. CRAIG

AIR + WATER = Sailing

Snapshot: Ocean spray and mist

Highlights: Intellectual, emotional, sensitive

Must-haves: The deeper needs of Air and Water can appear mutually exclusive. Air needs things to remain free and lighthearted, and Water needs emotional reassurance and deep feelings. This apparent opposition can actually result in a great benefit for each of you. Air can help Water become lighter in spirit, and Water can help Air become a person of greater depth.

The Pluses: A big draw in the Air/Water relationship is your ability to appreciate each other. While it takes some work to understand one another, the payoff makes the effort worthwhile. When you achieve a balance between logic and emotion, you become more harmonious as a couple and as individuals.

The effect that Air/Water has is to lighten up the heavy, emotional nature of Water and provide meaning to the vast knowledge of Air. Air helps Water see the funny side of life by taking the doom out of experiences, and Water offers Air a more profound view of facts, showing Air that there is a human impact behind all those stories we read.

There is admiration and appreciation of the differences at a truly profound level. So many occasions pop up in life that require an Air or Water talent. Is this situation better served by a more clinical or more sensitive approach? By having them both in the same partnership, a team forms that can take on the world.

The Minuses: Air/Water is a classic mind-heart conflict. As a result, this pair operates from a different approach to life. Mutual confusion represents the biggest challenge of the Air/Water connection. In many ways, you just don't understand each other at all.

Air lives primarily in the head and takes a logical approach in most situations. Water experiences life from a different perspective, relying not on facts and figures but on feelings and intuition. Too often the Air/Water conflict comes from doubting that the other person's "way" has any real validity.

Making matters worse, Air has a hard time with emotional needs, and Water is full of them. When the moment comes for Air to take time for themselves, watch out if Water is in the mood for snuggling on the couch or a chat about the day's upsets.

Air dislikes emotional drama and will leave the scene to avoid an argument. When Water gets upset, he or she wants to work it out. If Air tries to evade the argument by running off, Water will call Air's cell phone, and send a flood of text messages and emails. Water knows that Air is never without his or her communication tools. Trouble is, they have no problem ignoring them.

Air can consider Water's intuition and instinctive approach inferior to logic and hard evidence. This can make Air very distant if he or she doesn't feel safe in their thinking. When this happens, though, Water can feel isolated and believe that Air lacks depth as a human being.

The Challenge: Think of an avalanche: icy-cold Air and frozen Water cascading uncontrollably downhill. The issue here is to prevent such an event. When Air takes on an aloof and distant attitude, Water is first going to feel despondent. But as time goes by and Water feels increasingly emotionally isolated, an icy cold will freeze the intimacy in this relationship. This is a condition that only gets worse for Air/Water. The challenge is for Air to remain connected to Water's need for reassurances. Can you just listen to Water's angst without trying to fix it? If you can, sincere appreciation will quickly ensue.

Suggestion: One half of healing is laughter, and a comedy is what's on order for you. Rent the funniest video you've ever seen. Ask your social network community to recommend the funniest videos they've ever seen. Watch them all. Host a laugh-a-thon and be with each other until you both cry from amusement in each other's arms. Hug, kiss, and laugh some more.

In Private: When it comes to sex, the Air/Water couple knows how to communicate. Air loves to arouse Water with erotic talk, role-playing, and fantasy games. Plus, Water can slow you down a little, keeping you involved for longer with an emotional depth that lets you be more physically present. Instead of rushing off to the next thing, the enticing nature of Water's response keeps you focused. Air may get a chance to open up more with Water, allowing themselves to feel in places that aren't all that familiar.

In Public: When you find a midway point between logic and emotion and can dwell comfortably in both places, your relationship will bring you much joy. Air's cold logic needs Water's humanizing warmth, and Water needs Air's reasonable influence to avoid drowning in emotions. Once found, this balanced vibe shows. People think you're dynamic together, a balance of yin and yang. Air is witty and loves the facts, and Water is warm and adds color to expression. Together, you have the entire package. You make people think and feel good too—a rare combination.

Some Air/Water Advice

Dear Dr. Craig,

For six months, I've been dating a really wonderful girl. What's really special about her is the way she relates to my sister's kids. She's protective and really loving, telling them stories and making them feel cared for. I've been thinking about starting a family and feel that this woman might be the one. What concerns me is that everything is so intense for her. I'm pretty easygoing, but she can't even spill milk without it turning into a tragedy. How's she going to respond if something really big happens? I don't want to just shut down, because I really like this girl. Please advise.

—IT'S NOT THE HEAT, IT'S THE HUMIDITY

Dear Humid,

This lovely girl is a classic Water type. Feelings for her are really big, and emotional experiences can be scary. It's like trying to explain lightning to a child. You can offer reassurance by saying that lightning is electricity from the sky, or you can say lightning can fry people. When she's afraid, you can make it better simply by telling her it'll be okay. You're a lighthearted Air type, but you have to realize that not everything is fun and games. Even spilled milk might be worth crying over if it was the last glass, you really wanted it, and the convenience store was closed.

—DR. CRAIG

AIR + EARTH = Mutual benefits
Snapshot: Smooth landing
Highlights: Fun, practical, productive

Must-haves: At first glance, it might appear that Air and Earth could never meet each other's deeper needs. Air needs to feel free, unrestricted, and flexible. Earth needs stability, security, and structure. Can the twain ever meet? Absolutely! The Air/Earth combination can rock! Earth can help Air focus its energy and become more productive. And Air can help Earth lighten up and enjoy life more fully. It's not easy, but it's possible to find a balance that works for both of you.

The Pluses: Air and Earth know how to collaborate and produce results. Air often generates lots of information that drifts away as he or she moves on to the next thing. But Earth captures Air's thoughts, grounds them, and generates practical applications. The Air/Earth pair makes for a truly productive combination!

Add to the mix that Air brings abundant energy and curiosity and Earth brings capability and know-how, and you get a team that gets things done! Together, you can shop, renovate a house, and even diaper a baby. Air has the inquisitive mind to find the answer, and Earth has the wherewithal to do the task.

This brings about a great team, and a lot of trust can develop between you. Earth is not likely to restrict Air's movement. If Air wants to go out, take a class, or be a part of a social club, Earth is more than happy to let them have space.

The Minuses: The primary challenge in this relationship is a difference in tempo. Air zips from thing to thing and loves to multitask. Earth is methodical and must finish one thing before starting something else. In this relationship, Air could feel limited by Earth's rules, and Earth could feel disrupted by Air's lack of organization.

It's a question of priorities for the Air/Earth couple. Air loves freedom and Earth loves order. Freedom and order have never been close friends. Order requires that you follow a certain set of standards, rules, and behaviors. It doesn't have to be rigid, but Air feels it is.

Freedom requires space and spontaneity, and for Earth that could feel unsafe and frightening. Earth needs to have some things figured out. It's more difficult for him or her to venture out without knowing the consequences. This drives Air crazy.

Because Air and Earth have such different styles, you sometimes blame each other when things don't go your way. If Earth keeps driving around looking for a parking space, Air might blame Earth's slow pace for missed opportunities to get a spot. If Air forgets to pay a parking ticket, Earth can bemoan Air's flakiness and irresponsibility. The rapid and metered Air/Earth couple can have an exceedingly hard time blending.

The Challenge: Be aware when you're acting in a judgmental manner toward each other. Instead of judging, try to understand what's motivating the other person to behave in a particular way. Is Air feeling boxed in? Is Earth feeling unsteady? Air makes quick decisions, while Earth needs to think things over. If Air makes a hasty decision, Earth can get upset. If Earth refuses to make a timely decision, Air might get upset. How can you let your partner move at his or her own pace without being impatient or freaked out?

Suggestion: Do anything together that has instructions or a recipe. Bake health muffins. Make homemade pink lemonade. Rewire the home entertainment system. Plant something in the yard after reading its sun and water requirements. Then go enjoy the whole setup as one big harmonious moment.

In Private: Sex for the Air/Earth pair is active—even sweaty! While Air may take charge of most of the action, Earth has the staying power to make the experience memorable. Earth loves to lie back and enjoy the experience, and Air keeps things exciting with lots of activity and erotic talk. Air finds an amazing turn-on in his or her Earth partner: someone who has the capacity to receive physical attention in abundance and deliver tangible feedback with gusto!

In Public: You're a couple that gets things done. Air has the facts and data, and Earth knows how to bring abstract information into concrete reality. People view you as successful because you have the symbols of outward achievement plus the social status to give you real standing in your community. You can go before any community board and voice your opinion. Air is articulate and Earth is a reliable anchor. In fact, you might just end up on that community board yourselves.

Some Air/Earth Advice

Dear Dr. Craig,

My husband is driving me crazy. I am the flexible type. Anything goes with me, and I like it that way. Lately, though, he has been so rigid. Everything needs to be routine and deliber-

ate. I can't even leave my side of the bed untucked in the morning. I just want the freedom to do it my way. He has his own set of rules. We can't even go to the grocery without him bringing a big list and sticking to it. I've been with my husband for a long time, and I really love him, but he's got to loosen up. What on Earth should I do?

—PULLED TOO TIGHT

Dear Pulled,

Earth people need order; otherwise, they feel insecure. It sounds like your husband is an Earth type who's taken consistency to a new level. Before you start sleeping in separate beds, figure out how to meet him halfway. Tuck in the bedding when you get up and untuck it before you get into bed at night. Add a section to the grocery list called "I forgot to put it on the list." That way, if you see something, you can add it on the spot. Most of his concerns are about comfort and security. Maybe his grocery list is specific because he's trying to stay on a budget. Even though you're an Air type and not budget-conscious by nature, you need to appreciate your husband's concerns. You can probably get your man to loosen up if he knows you're financially responsible. Don't forget compromise. If you meet somewhere in the middle, I'd wager you're going to spend more time together in that untucked bed.

—DR. CRAIG

At the Café

Different couples respond to the same experience in different ways. Air loves cafés because they're great places to meet friends and have conversations. What happens when Air pairs up with other elements at a café? Let's take a look.

Air/Air Couple: This café one-to-one is a free-ranging discussion. When Air meets Air in the café, watch out. Your table may not be free for the rest of the day. The two of you can find so much to talk and laugh about that you'll stay on past closing time. The conversation might start with current events then move on to mutual friends, work, the art scene, doctor recommendations—you name it. You love to spend time together and never run out of things to talk about. Time spent together is time to read newspaper articles to each other, do the crossword, and check out the movie reviews.

Air/Fire Couple: This café encounter is a dialogue about ideas. Air and Fire love to let the inspiration flow along with the java. Fire enjoys brainstorming with Air because Air can articulate Fire's ideas and give them validity. Air and Fire manage to cover a lot of territory in a short period of time. The spark between them is so intense, they can take an idea and run with it. While you may only spend an hour together tossing opinions around, you've managed to get more done than most people accomplish in an entire day.

Air/Water Couple: This café meeting is a heart-to-heart chat. When Air and Water get together, you'll discuss personal situations, family matters, pressing concerns, puzzling problems, and all things near and dear to you. Because Air has a clear, logical mind, Water can count on Air to listen and help sort things out. Air can look to Water for empathy, acceptance, and understanding. Your connection is rich and deep. On the positive side, sharing pictures and stories from a recent vacation is just the right Air/Water pastime. If things are tough, there's more than enough concern to make for a meaningful discussion.

Air/Earth Couple: This café get-together is a bit more practical. When Air and Earth meet, Air finally has a place to really discuss the news and Earth loves bringing the discussion close to home. How's the market doing? And what's going on with this baseball season? This makes the Air/Earth café substantial. Earth could be helping a friend find an apartment and asks Air to recommend a rental agent, which Air readily provides. Air mentions an ongoing job search, and Earth offers to review Air's résumé to make sure it packs a punch. In this way, the talk flows back and forth, with each of you offering practical assistance and problem solving.

16
Water in the Mix

WATER + WATER = Deep feelings

Snapshot: Sentimental journey

Highlights: Sensitive, intuitive, emotional

Must-haves: Since you're both Water types, you have the same deeper needs in a relationship. You need to feel understood and honored on an emotional level. You also want to feel reassured, cared for, and protected. For this relationship to work, don't get so wrapped up in your own emotional interplay that you lose sight of the world outside of your feelings.

The Pluses: The biggest draw of the Water/Water relationship is that you understand each other on a profound, emotional level. What a relief! Finally, someone who doesn't make you feel unstable, overly sensitive, weepy, or whiny. Your partner appreciates that same emotional validation too.

Being comfortable with feelings, you aren't threatened by each other's emotional reactions. Whether it's happy, sad, or somewhere in between, you both really know how to empathize. When life is positive, you can count on that big, supportive reaction. When negative, the Water/Water couple truly feels for each other. Sympathy and understanding are sincere, and a comforting hug is there at the ready.

What comes easily in this relationship is the way you communicate on an intuitive level. You don't need to even speak. You can sense what the other is feeling and thinking. There is rarely, if ever, a time when you feel misunderstood, and this feels like a real novelty.

The Water/Water pair finds similar interests and compatible reactions in living. Cry at the same TV commercials? Belly-laugh at the same spot in a movie? Together, you are suited to enjoying life in a like-feeling way. The tingles never have to stop for a Water couple; they keep right on flowing!

The Minuses: Empathy is great, but too much empathy can have a negative effect. You can get caught in an emotional spiral where you can't stop feeling sad, depressed, or grief-filled. As a pair, you can drown in your emotions if you don't find a way to stabilize your feelings or remain grounded.

Arguments usually occur when one or both of you get stuck in negative emotions. Maybe this happened because neither one of you is that good with staying on top of the bills. When this happens, you may blame one another for what you're feeling. One of you may play the martyr. Instead of realizing that your emotionally based world needs a little contact with reality, you may drift off and wallow in further fantasy and emotional recrimination.

The relationship is in dangerous territory when emotions run your life and you've lost perspective. While it's uplifting to understand each other's emotions, it can end up being destructive to escape from emotional overload. Escapism of all kinds, whether in front of the TV or a super-size-me jolly meal, is not going to make the harder feelings better.

The Challenge: Watch out for negativity. You could be so focused on heavy emotions that you begin to see only the dark, sad side of life. If you focus on the negative, your relationship can degenerate into a pity party. Try to set limits. How can you visit your heavier feelings without becoming stuck in them? Maybe you need time to feel sadness or other challenging emotions but could gently tell each other when enough is enough.

Suggestion: Take an art class together. Go to one of those pottery art workshops where you can buy a ready-made piece and paint it yourself. Or go to the art supply store and look around together. Express yourselves in a creative, artistic way and feel the love.

In Private: Sex for the Water/Water couple is more than a physical experience. It's an expression of a deep emotional, even spiritual, connection. By being so in tune with each other, you know right where to go and what to do. You're relaxed and comfortable, and this makes you feel more open and less vulnerable than with other types. Perhaps you'd like to take it slow, explore each other to the fullest, and connect on the deepest levels. You love nothing more than to spend plenty of time cuddling, snuggling, and hugging. If you could, the Water/Water combination would squeeze each other until they finally merged as one.

In Public: Water/Water couples are gentle and caring with each other. People feel your warm, loving partnership and admire your closeness, empathy, and strong bond. You feel safe expressing yourself emotionally around others and can spend hours together laughing and crying. You are partners in the heart's journey toward feeling, and everyone can see it! Because you're sentimental and love customs, traditions, and nostalgia, you are often the couple with a festive holiday party and an annual Girl Scout fundraiser.

Some Water/Water Advice

Dear Dr. Craig,

Our cat died about three months ago. My wife and I had him for fifteen years, and now my wife has become really, really sad. I've been sad too—don't get me wrong. But my wife's been going over all our old photos and still can't put away his toys. It feels like a dark cloud is hanging over the house. My wife and I are so close. We don't even need to talk; we just know how we're feeling. But I'm having such a hard time spending time with her these days. I don't know how to snap her out of it. What do you suggest?

—GOING UNDER

Dear Under,

Letting go is hard, especially with a beloved friend. Grieving is a very private matter. We all grieve in our own time. Still, for two Water types, there is the danger of getting lost in emotional intensity. Your wife doesn't want to lose sight of your love for your pet. But moving on is important. You can do that by making sure you've said good-bye with a meaningful ritual. I'm sure your wife will welcome the chance to honor your beloved cat. Tell stories, laugh a little, and try to lighten up the mood with some uplifting music. Then put away most of the reminders and suggest that it's time to let go. Your wife will come around. She just needs to feel the depth of her pain and know that you feel it too.

—DR. CRAIG

WATER + FIRE = Emotional intensity

Snapshot: Depth charge

Highlights: Enthusiastic, sensitive, imaginative

Must-haves: Water is attracted to Fire's big personality, and Fire is drawn to Water's big feelings. While the attraction can be strong, it won't last long unless each of you meets the other's deeper needs. Water needs emotional validation, reassurance, and protection. Fire needs to feel important and creative and receive recognition and praise. While you come from different places, you can learn to appreciate each other's different styles.

The Pluses: Water's emotions are aroused in the presence of Fire's larger-than-life energy. Fire feels validated by Water's emotional responsiveness. Together, you can transform one another. Water can bring Fire greater emotional depth, and Fire can bring Water greater emotional creativity.

When Water and Fire come together, there is a passion for life. Real magic happens because enthusiasm and feelings merge to create exciting and meaningful events. Even cooking dinner together produces a meal that is original and sublime.

What comes naturally in the Water/Fire relationship is the romance and adventure you inspire in each other. Water and Fire are both intensely romantic. Water may write a love poem for Fire about winter, and Fire in turn whisks Water away for a surprise trip to a ski lodge. Because Water is so receptive to Fire's ideas, there is a drive in Fire to keep delivering more.

The Minuses: The two of you can overwhelm each other. Water's emotions can drown out Fire, and Fire's intensity can dry up Water. Water needs Fire to allow room for feelings. Fire needs Water to allow room for Fire itself. Finding that happy medium and setting up a lasting relationship is going to be a task.

At a certain point, Fire is going to feel like Water's emotional needs are a downer—too much preoccupation with the heavy, feelings-based drama of your relationship, family, and friends. Why does it always have to be so intense? This is Fire's lament with Water as a long-term partner.

Water in turn ends up feeling that Fire doesn't care. You may listen endlessly to Fire's enthusiastic rants about his or her day, plans, and vision, and then when it comes time for a little emotional sharing on your part, there's nothing in return. This makes Water feel really sad, misunderstood, and, worse yet, unloved!

You're on dangerous ground when you begin to feel like a lesser version of yourself. This happens when Fire and Water neutralize each other. Water can feel evaporated by too much exposure to Fire, feeling there's no room for emotional expression. Fire can feel drowned out by Water's perceived emotional excess. If you don't feel like yourself anymore, there won't be a way for this couple to last.

The Challenge: Realizing just how different you really are is the work of the Water/Fire pair. Sometimes Water just wants to stay at home and snuggle by the TV, while Fire wants to go out on the town. And that's just the beginning of having really alternate approaches to the situations of life. Can you be more upbeat or more sympathetic to the nature of your partner's approach to life? When you see that each of you has a valuable way of viewing the world, your Water/Fire relationship transforms you both.

Suggestion: Go dancing! When was the last time you did that? If you think you're no good at dancing, you don't have to be "good." Just go for the fun of it, for the laughs. Be creative. Be expressive. You'll be surprised at how much rhythm the two of you can muster up on the dance floor, and who knows where that will lead?

In Private: When Water mixes with Fire, expect some steamy sex. Fire is the most sexually creative style you will ever encounter. That poses a big range of feelings for Water. Do you want it naughty? Do you want it nice? All these complex feelings, and Fire is the one who knows how to bring them out in you. And Water should never think that those feeling go unnoticed—not in bed. Fire loves the reinforcement that Water provides; the feedback is palpable to Fire and makes the moment even hotter.

In Public: Water and Fire can be each other's biggest fans. You stimulate one another and take each other places where you'd never go alone. Others are attracted to you, proving that opposites do indeed attract. You are enthusiastic storytellers, enjoying the moments when you can share your adventures with friends. Water adds deep feelings to Fire's intensity, and Fire adds passion to Water's colorful imagination. Together, you always climb the highest mountain, visit the newest exhibit, and catch the big fish.

Some Water/Fire Advice

Dear Dr. Craig,

I've been going out with my boyfriend for about a year. He's awesome. All my friends tell me I've got a winner. I love that. We do a lot of things together because he is always planning something fun. One thing that's not fun, though, is that he doesn't validate my stories. He's always got to top me. It's like no matter what I have to say, he always knows more, has had a more incredible experience, or is bored with what I told him.

This hurts my feelings. I mean, I've got some good stories to tell. How am I going to make some room for myself with him?

—*SMALLER THAN LIFE*

Dear Smaller,

First of all, you are not smaller than life. You are just in the shadow of this very big Fire type. It can be hard to get him to understand your feelings, and, as a Water type, you sound like someone who has very sweet feelings. After all, your experiences are big for you, and this boyfriend is going to be one big fish to fry. I'm talking about getting him to appreciate your need for expression! Try to teach him how to say "Wow." He may not be impressed by anything other than himself, but if you can teach him to say "Wow," he'll come around. You'll show him that you can be pretty lively too.

—DR. CRAIG

WATER + AIR = Rhyme and reason

Snapshot: Effervescence

Highlights: Imaginative, emotional, logical

Must-haves: Water and Air's deeper needs can seem like a study in opposites. Water needs someone to validate his or her emotional depth, while Air flees from heavy emotions and needs to remain lighthearted. Water wants to feel cared for and reassured, and Air needs to keep things flexible and free. Can Water and Air meet each other's needs? Yes! And each can become more balanced and multidimensional in the process!

The Pluses: Water can always count on Air for a much-needed good laugh. Life can be so burdensome, and Air has an easy, natural way of making it lighter. This helps Water's serious mood and puts things in perspective. If the world can be looked at with humor and acceptance, why does it need to be so heavy? Water gains space around emotions with Air, making them more manageable and less overwhelming.

Air also encourages Water to articulate his or her feelings. This allows Water to examine his or her emotions in a calm, productive manner. There's less use for hysteria and emotional overload when Water is with Air. Bigger emotions don't make a bigger impact on Air, so a clear expression of feelings is usually enough.

For Air, the connection to Water brings warmth into a life that could remain cold and cerebral. Too much time in the intellect can make Air an unfeeling style. Water adds that bit of humanness to Air that otherwise might get neglected.

The Minuses: When the Water/Air relationship is out of balance, confusion results. You don't know where the other person is coming from. Water relies on intuition, and Air relies on logic. You may make each other feel wrong about how you approach life, believing your way is superior. But no single way is the "best."

If Water feels that Air is emotionally dismissive or distant, an argument often crops up. But when Air senses an emotional scene or drama coming on, it takes off. Dealing with an argument is difficult with such different styles. Water needs to listen to Air's rational dis-section of the problem, and Air needs to understand how Water may feel a certain way. But doing that is easier said than done.

Water needs caring and warmth and is sensitive to any lack of feeling or coldness from Air. This will cause Water to withdraw and feel wounded, even if Air was merely preoccupied and not intention-ally dismissive. If Water becomes clingy and needy of emotional sup-port, Air runs further into personal space and distance. Feeling separate is a hard place to connect from.

The Challenge: Watch out for frustration. Water can get frustrated with Air's insistence on rational proof. "How do you know that?" Air might ask. "I just know," Water responds. When Air presses for more information, Water can shut down and tune out. Air can get frustrated with Water's big emotional reactions, even to minor occurrences, and can ignore or trivialize Water's feelings. Can you strike a balance between thinking and feeling? When might a few additional facts actually be helpful? Bringing together the head and heart is not easy, but you can do it.

Suggestion: Try a romantic dinner. Make a reservation at a small, warmly lit place that serves just the foods you love. Have a real conversation together about the last time you went away for the weekend. Discuss what you each liked best. Reminisce about the details, and then plan your next getaway.

In Private: Water and Air can have lots of fun in bed. Water is imaginative and loves fantasy, and Air is verbal and loves to play-act. Together, you can devise scenarios that will stimulate and satisfy both of you. There is plenty of room for nonjudgmental role play. Water ends up having some of his or her deeper, private fantasies acted out in a safe way, while Air acts out those same fantasies with a free and experimental quality that keeps Water smiling.

In Public: Water represents the heart, and Air represents the mind. As a couple, when you share your essence with each other, Water gains rational perspective on his or her emotions, and Air gains emotional insights into his or her thoughts. Other people respond to your heart/mind connection and think of you as a couple that knows how to express what you're feeling. You've taught that to each other, and it shows. You come across as a couple with dueling perspectives that has learned to bridge the gap.

Some Water/Air Advice

Dear Dr. Craig,

My wife is one of the funniest people I know. She is always making me laugh. I love her sense of humor, but sometimes she doesn't seem to know when enough is enough. The other day, I banged my head so hard that I thought I was seeing stars. She started laughing. She said that it looked so funny in a slapstick way that she just couldn't help herself. I felt really angry, and I still feel hurt. I feel like I got hit in the head twice! What's up with that?

—ONE OR TWO LUMPS

Dear Lumpy,

You are clearly a Water type, and your feelings matter. Trouble is, your wife is an Air type, and humor is a way that she copes. Sympathy in the moment is not one of her strong points. You like her ability to lighten things up, but that doesn't always work when you feel fragile. Still, the ice pack belongs on your noggin and not on your heart! Don't forget to express yourself to her. She needs that extra bit of sensitive information to keep her awareness of your feelings. I'm sure when she realizes you're hurting in a couple of places, she'll come around and you can laugh about it together.

—DR. CRAIG

WATER + EARTH = Safe haven

Snapshot: Comfort zone

Highlights: Imaginative, dependable, caring

Must-haves: Water and Earth are extremely compatible and represent a natural pair. Water has a deeper need to feel cared for and nurtured, and Earth offers safety and dependability. Earth needs stability and security, and Water offers the emotional openness that lets Earth know where he or she stands. Together, there is a harmony that soothes your partner's deeper needs.

The Pluses: You're drawn to each other by your love of art and your complementary talents for artistic expression. Water imagines the design, and Earth brings the concept to life. This makes any project or venture look effortless. With Water's vision and Earth's know-how, the fun is in making dreams come to life.

The Water/Earth pair works well with and on each other. You have the amazing effect of opening each other up and feeling truly respected. Water is less quick to judge, and Earth really appreciates the patience that Water is capable of, while Earth has an enormous capacity for Water's emotional states and provides a steady, available container for Water's feelings.

This allows each of you to unfold. Water connects with their intuition more solidly, and Earth manifests in the world with more depth. In a space of comfort, the Water/Earth couple brings enduring creation to life. You don't just build a house together; you build a lasting home.

The Minuses: A pitfall of the Water/Earth relationship is that you can become too attached. An unhealthy fusion and clinginess takes over when you don't feel complete without one another. You don't want to disagree or challenge the status quo because you're afraid of losing your partner, and a relationship based on fear isn't healthy.

You need to maintain a sense of openness so you can honestly discuss what's going on. When Water tries to change Earth's mind about something and Earth refuses to budge, an argument is in the offing. Water can feel as if Earth is acting difficult for no reason. Earth can get annoyed when Water lays on a guilt trip to get his or her way. When Water and Earth are at an impasse, Water will wallow in emotions and Earth will retreat to chores and mundane endeavors. Realize that you're not trying to hurt each other on purpose. Earth is naturally methodical and orderly. If Earth decides on a best approach, Water can do little to change Earth's mind. Still, Earth needs to consider that Water may have a valid point. If you can keep the lines of communication open, you will prevent turning misunderstandings into full-scale disagreements.

Water and Earth need to watch out for too much togetherness. If you're not careful, you can lose your individuality and become overly attached. Keep a healthy balance in your relationship by doing things together and developing individual interests.

The Challenge: Water loves to flow and can get frustrated if Earth remains too rigid. But when Earth thinks that a practical solution overrides an emotional concern, look out! Earth refuses to bend and remains stubborn, and Water lets loose with drama. While Earth is normally sympathetic to Water's emotions, when there's reality to consider, Earth tunes out. Earth can say, "That's the way it is." In turn, Water gets even more emotional to elicit a response from Earth. The cycle continues, and each becomes entrenched in his or her own "rightness." When a practical solution is in order, can you admit it to yourself? Living in a real world is not always easy for Water, but when the time and place are right, try it; Earth will be there to comfort you.

Suggestion: Nature! The beach, the mountains, or the local creek trail; they are all waiting for you. Plan a picnic; make it simple. Bring just what you need for a fine afternoon in a park or other natural setting. Maybe even bring along a little radio for added ambience. And bring the camera! You are both going to want to capture the memories.

In Private: Sex for the Water/Earth couple is extremely sensual. Water instinctively knows how to please Earth, and Earth loves every second of it. Lovemaking for you is unrushed and enjoyable, warm, and fulfilling. There is plenty of time for back rubs, foot rubs, and any kind of rubs for that matter. Taking a bath together is delightful, and after-bath play with chocolate sauce is heaven. Earth is the reliable, comforting teddy bear of love, which makes Water feel fulfilled.

In Public: Water and Earth make a stunning match. Together you're artistic, multitalented, and able to bring your vision to life. Water can have a softening influence on Earth, making him or her less rigid. In turn, Earth grounds Water's emotions. This natural partnership brings happiness on many levels. Other people enjoy your company because you're so well balanced and easygoing. They see the warmth, humanity, and refinement. The Water/Earth couple shows the world a healthy, emotional connection, a love of art, physical warmth, and the practical application of their vision.

Some Water/Earth Advice

Dear Dr. Craig,

I'm dating a great guy. He's reliable and very old-fashioned in a way that I like. My life is pretty busy. I've got my job, which is always a source of tension, and I've got my parents and their drama. I have plenty on my plate. Last week, I met my guy for a lovely walk in the park. We had a lot of privacy, and I wanted so much to talk to him. But things didn't turn out the way I'd hoped. I felt like I wanted to just have someone listen to me. Instead, he wanted to fix everything for me. He said there was a practical solution to every problem. I'm not sure that works for me. What do you think?

—DON'T FIX ME

Dear Unfixed,

When you've got a lot going on, it can be emotionally over-whelming. You sound like a Water type, and you need someone who will simply understand what you're going through with-out trying to make it better. This new guy is an Earth type. He's dependable but also results oriented. You can't blame him for wanting to find a solution. He sees you're stressed and wants to help. You need to tell him that it's about your feelings, about what's going on behind your work and family drama. And that doesn't need fixing! It just needs a hug and a reliable listener. As an Earth type, he can be that!

—DR. CRAIG

At the Movie Theater

Different people respond to the same experience in different ways. Water loves art and enjoys going to the movies. Let's see what happens when Water attends a movie with other elemental types.

Water/Water Couple: This movie viewing is an emotional experience. When two Water types see a film together, you can empathize with the characters and feel free about expressing your emotions. You will probably laugh and cry at the same spots. If one is more emotionally overtaken, the other will offer comfort with an arm around the shoulder. Afterward, you don't need to say a word. You each know exactly what the other felt about the film. The movie can provide a cathartic experience for both of you.

Water/Fire Couple: This trip to the flicks is a creative experience. When Water and Fire attend a movie together, the viewing is enthusiastic and emotional. Fire gets excited about the ideas the movie inspires. Water merges with the film emotionally, from the atmosphere to the plight of the characters and every other nuance of feeling. By sharing different perspectives, Water and Fire enhance each other's enjoyment of the film.

Water/Air Couple: This film screening is an intellectual experience. When Water and Air go to a movie together, it may take time to pick something you both want to see. Air loves comedies, and Water wants drama, from sadness to fright. When you agree on which movie, Water will focus on the sensitive, emotional aspects of the production while Air will key in on the language and dialogue of the film. Afterward, Air amazes Water with his or her ability to recall minor details of the story and recite dialogue verbatim. Water will share insights about the emotional aspects of the film and recount subtle aspects of meaning that Air completely missed. Together, they gain deeper insight.

Water/Earth Couple: This movie outing is an artistic and emotional experience. Water and Earth love the art of cinema and look forward to enjoying an uplifting experience. You will probably hold hands throughout the film! Water gets so caught up in the story that he or she sometimes needs emotional support. Earth is happy to assist! Water's emotional attunement enhances Earth's enjoyment of the film by putting him or her in touch with their own emotions. While watching the movie, Earth notices production values, period details, and historical accuracy. Water notes whether the acting is believable; if not, the whole film can fall flat. By sharing, Water and Earth enhance their deep appreciation for the movie.

17
Earth in the Mix

Earth + Earth = Rock solid

Snapshot: Bankable pair

Highlights: Dependable, loyal, steady

Must-haves: Earth types have a deep need to feel safe. You want stability in your life and expect others to act responsibly and keep their commitments. More than anything, you crave security. A steady, structured life in comfortable surroundings is a must. Fortunately, you've found another Earth type—someone who desires a steady life just as much as you do. You really share common ground!

The Pluses: The biggest draw of this relationship is that you can depend on each other. You're both equally concerned with security and work together to create a stable, reliable lifestyle. This means you're on the same page when it comes to saving money, living within your means, and enjoying a warm, comfortable home. The Earth/ Earth pair most definitely builds the brick house.

When Earth merges with Earth, you get twice the dependability, and together, you rock! You find it easy to trust each other. This is such a relief! With complete faith in one another's loyalty, you feel safe and secure. It's as if a burden has been lifted. For Earth, finding someone with similar concerns is one of the greatest finds in life.

Because your partnership results in mutual confidence, you can invest your energy in practical matters, such as building an addition on the house, your bank account, and a life together. The Earth/Earth couple is durable. You stand the test of time, weathering adversity with your steadfast endurance and attention to quality.

The Minuses: The problem with all that dependability is that it can sometimes get predictable to the point of monotony. You need to watch out for getting so wrapped up in mundane details that you forget to look up and see the stars. Romance and practicality can mix. Just think of all the money you'll save on electricity if you light some candles every once in a while.

Earth types are quiet and low-key, so you're not prone to loud arguments, or any arguments for that matter. Complacent behavior is another downside to the Earth/Earth couple. Even when there's a problem going on for one of you, it may not get voiced until it's too late. Being okay with the status quo is a real danger for you.

Watch out that too much relaxation and comfort don't result in you feeling bogged down and bored. Even though a slow, steady pace suits you both, it is possible that you want more. If an Earth-Earth combination presents no challenge, you will become disinterested. Security is the foundation of your realities, but all work and no play makes Earth—well, you know.

The Challenge: Your strong bond is based in large part on your mutual desire for stability. You have mutual funds and sensible cars and get your teeth cleaned at least twice a year. You love to balance the checkbook together and get excited about each other's raise or promotion. This is fine as far as it goes. But you need to make sure there is more to your relationship than just the material aspects. Your feet are on the ground, but can you slip into some dancing shoes every once in a while?

Suggestion: Get off the couch! Go for a walk. Hold hands and walk around your neighborhood. Look for flowers or changes in the season. Take deep breaths. Give each other frequent hugs. Really take in your environment with your senses. This could turn out to be very stimulating for both of you.

In Private: You love to get cozy and warm with each other and are masters at cuddling, hugging, and snuggling. Your sex life is steady and dependable. When it's time to make love, you can count on each other for a warm, loving, sensual experience. Body to body contact feels so good, and sometimes it's more about the touching than the sex. It feels safe when you're together, and you totally trust each other on the physical as well as every other level.

In Public: Earth types need status and esteem from others. As an Earth couple, you both care about the same things and would never jeopardize your social standing. People view you as upstanding citizens and pillars of the community. You get involved in local activities, serving on boards of associations, schools, and museums. Whenever people need a helping hand, you are there to pitch in, get things organized, and make life better for everyone. Your strong bond and commitment to each other makes it easy for you to share with family, friends, and your neighborhood.

Some Earth/Earth Advice

Dear Dr. Craig,

My husband and I have been together for eight years. I've known him since we were kids. He's terrific. I can really count on him. Years ago, we opened a joint checking account. At the time, we agreed to ask each other before using money from the account. Well, last week he went into the account without asking me. He said we needed a new smoke detector for the house and didn't think he needed to get my permission. I'm trying to understand why he did it, but I can't get it out of my head that he broke our agreement. Am I wrong?

—STILL SMOLDERING

Dear Smoldering,

Sounds like you two Earth types could use a little appreciation of each other's assets. I think you're right. If you had an agreement, he should stick to it. After all, for you to feel secure, he has to be dependable. To that point, he sounds like a rock. In this recent case, he was concerned about the household's safety. That's a good thing. Now that he knows how you feel about the joint account, he's unlikely to go into it again without talking to you first. Look at his intentions. He was acting responsibly. Maybe what he did doesn't feel minor to you. That's okay. But dipping into your joint account to pay for a smoke detector may have been one of the best mistakes he's ever made.

—DR. CRAIG

EARTH + FIRE = Creative production

Snapshot: Steady heat

Highlights: Productive, enthusiastic, reliable

Must-haves: Earth has a deep need for security and reliability and wants a steady, dependable partner. Fire has a different agenda—one that values creative expression over earthly possessions. Can the two of you find common ground? No question about it. In fact, Earth and Fire can make a great team! Earth has the practical skills and know-how to bring Fire's ideas to life. You stimulate each other's sense of adventure and lead each other to new experiences.

The Pluses: Earth can handle Fire's heat. Fire often moves so fast that many of his or her good ideas just fade away. But Earth knows how to capture all that creativity and transform it into a useful form. Fire may come up with a recipe, but Earth knows how to turn it into a meal. Together, Earth and Fire can bring ideas into being.

What comes easily in this relationship is a creative flow, from conception to birth. It feels natural to make things happen together. Earth appreciates Fire's sense of adventure and feels revitalized by Fire's creative spirit. Fire marvels at how Earth can point out where an idea is lacking practicality. This is an important contribution to the creative process, as it eliminates unrealistic wastes of time.

Fire may know how to plan exciting trips, but Earth understands how to get safely to the destination. The combination ensures safety and excitement. The thrill of an awesome, fast luxury car is something you both love, but Earth remembers to buckle up and bring safety to the ride.

The Minuses: While Earth and Fire make terrific creative partners, you have to work at other aspects of your relationship. Your natural rhythms are different and you move at different speeds. Earth likes a slow and steady pace, while Fire has only one speed: fast.

You may try to change each other, but you won't get too far. Earth feels insecure if he or she has to move too quickly, and Fire feels frustrated if he or she has to slow down too much. Finding the middle ground is not easy for the Earth/Fire couple.

Some of the difference in speed comes from Fire's excitement and Earth's easy attitude. Fire wants to feel the energy of life, while Earth wants to feel his or her favorite spot on the sofa. For Earth, just being surrounded by familiar, beautiful surroundings is enough. But Fire wants adventure, action, and to be seen.

If Fire feels bored with Earth, then there's going to be a seething time bomb. A lack of enthusiasm is like death to Fire, and a change would quickly be in order. When Earth feels Fire can't just stop for a minute and chill out, Earth gets agitated. This is another recipe for relationship demise. Earth types need calm, and the disruption that Fire could bring won't let that last very long.

The Challenge: For Earth types, downtime is a necessity, not a luxury. Sometimes Fire types can't understand why Earth needs so much time to relax. Fire may see Earth's hours spent decompressing as a waste or even pure laziness. "Come on, let's do something," Fire might say. When Earth begs off, Fire feels let down and takes Earth's refusal personally. How can you keep your energy high enough without feeling burnt? Take a look at all that rest and relaxation. Maybe a night on the town is all the relaxation you need.

Suggestion: Go to the theater, movies, or a music venue. Show off! Make it as high energy or as low-key as you like, but be in public. Dress up for it, even if that means just putting on a clean shirt. Make it a date! You will both have fun feeling proud and happy.

In Private: The Earth/Fire couple is a sensual, physical pair that loves to sleep wrapped around each other au naturel. Who needs a blanket when there are two hot bodies in bed? But the love doesn't stop with sleeping. Willing to experience most anything once, Earth is erotic putty in Fire's creative hands. Fire longs to have a willing partner who feels safe in his or her skin. Together, you can go where no two have gone before.

In Public: People look at the Earth/Fire couple and think, "Those two really know how to make things happen." In your community, you are movers and shakers. You come up with ideas and have the follow-through to bring them into reality. You're a great example of synergy, and your relationship makes each of you more productive than you would be alone. The Earth/Fire couple gets the job done. From start to finish, you earn the gratitude of yourselves and the people around you.

Some Earth/Fire Advice

Dear Dr. Craig,

My wife is an amazing woman. She lights up a room, and I always get a charge out of her. But lately she's been charging things up too much, and I'm talking about our credit cards. Since our daughter was born, it's gotten worse. My wife says she needs new clothes for herself and our daughter and new things for the house. I'm not cheap or selfish, but I think this has gone too far. My wife's spending is constant, and I think it's impulsive. To pay for all this, I'm afraid I'll have to mortgage the house. I need her to respect my plans for our future. We've got to think ahead. I'm a patient guy, but I'm losing it.

—FEELING SPENT

Dear Spent,

It sounds as if you're dealing with a reckless situation. But you need to stay calm. You're an Earth type. That means you're all about stability. Your wife is a clear Fire type, and it sounds like she's out of control. To contain a volatile situation, you're going to have to draw a fire line—the kind they use to prevent forest fires from spreading. By this, I'm telling you to set limits. Put your wife on a budget. Before you cancel all the cards, put yours on the table and tell her you feel the family is on shaky ground. Appeal to her innovative nature and see if she can get what she needs on less money. Maybe she can let those credit cards cool off while she chills out.

—DR. CRAIG

Earth + Air = Dependable fun

Snapshot: A knee-slapper

Highlights: Grounded, sociable, practical

Must-haves: Earth is tangible, and his or her deeper needs center on practical concerns: safety, security, dependability. Air is intangible, and his or her deeper needs revolve around breaking free from earthly restrictions and gaining freedom and flexibility. It seems as if Earth and Air wouldn't have much in common. But you do! Earth and Air can find a midway point and help each other see the other side of life. In this mutually beneficial pairing, Earth brings Air stability and Air brings Earth spontaneity.

The Pluses: The Earth/Air relationship works because you bolster each other. Earth helps Air become more grounded and centered, and

Air helps Earth become more lighthearted and curious. By sharing your strengths, you make one another stronger.

Together, you can turn intangible thoughts into tangible things. With Air providing their huge base of knowledge and Earth bringing in the can-do expertise, it's like having an instruction manual for life built right into the relationship. Together, you make it seem so easy!

As a result, laughter comes easily to the Earth/Air couple. You always have some inside joke. Air is so quick, and Earth retains the experiences of the past. Just the right glance or key phrase can set off a barrage of laughs. This kind of laughter builds an enduring foundation for your relationship—Earth continually admiring Air's quick wit and Air admiring the way Earth responds with such contented and deep-seated appreciation.

The Minuses: As you travel through life together, you'll have to reach a compromise about your rate of speed. Earth feels safer moving at a slow, steady pace, and Air feels freer moving at quick, unpredictable speeds. To prevent driving one another crazy, find ways to accommodate each other's preferences. Earth can step on the gas at times without worrying about going off the road, and Air can put on the brakes without losing any freedom. Together, you help each other move outside your comfort zones. Earth and Air would rather avoid an argument. Sometimes you get annoyed with each other because of your different styles. Earth thinks Air is irresponsible and won't heed good advice, and Air thinks Earth is bullheaded and won't listen to reason. If you push each other too far, one of you may get angry, though you might not admit it. Each of you are masters at going off by yourself, getting away from the problem, and not discussing what's bothering you. For the relationship to remain healthy, you have to open up and express what you're feeling. This kind of openness might not feel comfortable at first, but in the end it can bring you closer.

Sometimes you're driving along and you open the window, and the wind blows dust into your eyes. In a way, that's the nature of the Earth/Air conflict. Air likes to keep things moving but can blow up dust, making it hard to see down the road. Earth prefers to keep the windows safely closed, but, along with the dust, you'd miss the fresh air. Realize that you will irritate each other at times just because you're different. Wipe away the dust, look each other straight in the eyes, and realize that it's okay to bother each other from time to time. If you can laugh at your foibles, you'll prevent a little dust-up from turning into a sandstorm.

The Challenge: Earth is steady and methodical, so he or she can consider Air's flexibility and lack of structure as disorderly and confused. Free-spirited Air can view Earth's orderly methods as plodding. Can you be more allowing of the freedom and loose structure that will be necessary for this relationship to succeed? A kite may seem free, but really it's still tethered. Let go and follow it; you may find unrealized treasure in its path.

Suggestion: Find a group in your area. It could be spiritual, political, or involved in your community in some way. Go for one meeting or event. See what it's about. Create a larger circle of friends and activities that you both like. It could even be poker night at the local pizza restaurant.

In Private: When making love, Earth loves to feel skin and dissolve in a total sensual experience. Air knows how to satisfy Earth physically and asks that Earth return the favor with some mental stimulation. While Earth is relatively easy to satisfy, Air requires more work in this pair. Air wants variety, role-playing, and verbal interplay, and a few grunting noises may not be enough. Earth needs to keep things exciting or Air will lose interest. A healthy sex life means doing what turns on your partner! In this case, that means talk!

In Public: Earth and Air have a lot to offer and learn from each other. Earth helps Air stay focused, and Air helps Earth enjoy life more fully. Other people see you as well rounded and well grounded. Together, you're the warehouse of think tanks, the couple that can field an idea and come up with a solution that works. Your enjoyment of wide-ranging discussions often produces clever new approaches, and others seek you out for advice and counsel.

Some Earth/Air Advice

Dear Dr. Craig,

I've been dating a woman for about five months. I find her fascinating. She's got so much to say. And she's read so many cool things. Plus she makes me laugh, and I love that. I'm a hard-working guy, and I need time off to just relax and slow down. But my girlfriend is always on the go. When we're together, we go here, go there, and are doing something every minute. She can hardly watch a movie from beginning to end. Her schedule gets so filled that I wonder if we can ever find some downtime together. Can we work this out?

—GOING TOO FAST

Dear Fast,

Never a dull moment with an Air type, that's for sure. And that sounds like exactly what's going on for you. Love is great, but this isn't what it means to get blown away! Your girlfriend needs lots of activity. That can be good, because you'll never get bored. But for an Earth type like you, too much bustling around can feel disruptive. You need order or you feel spread too thin. Try to find activities that can hold her attention while giving you some R & R. Learn what kinds of movies she enjoys. Be prepared to watch chick flicks to get some serenity back in your life. Spend time reading to each other. Do some cooking together. See if she can slow down long enough to appreciate terra firma.

—DR. CRAIG

EARTH + WATER = Structural integrity

Snapshot: The artist's canvas

Highlights: Secure, imaginative, safe

Must-haves: Earth meets an ideal match in Water. It feels natural and easy to offer one another what you deeply need. Earth needs dependability and structure, and Water provides the emotional openness that keeps the relationship on solid ground. Water needs to feel cared for and nurtured, and Earth is a natural caregiver. The relationship feels so right. You're elated to be together.

The Pluses: It's quite normal for an Earth/Water couple to want to spend virtually every moment in each other's arms. The amazing part is how well you fit together—something you've seldom, if ever, experienced before. You feel safe and at ease sharing yourselves, body, mind, and soul. In fact, the longer you're together, the more you believe that you're a perfect match.

Earth finds it easy to open up to Water and even finds itself less rigid under Water's influence. Knowing that Water's got their back makes Earth feels a lot less restricted. Water feels secure and relaxed with Earth and is relieved to have found a trustworthy partner. There's no need to put tabs on an Earth lover; you always know where he or she is and what they're doing.

The Earth/Water pair shares the experience of the physical world in a compatible way. The sounds of the beach, the feel of the sand, and the excellent, extra-crispy fries from the snack vendor all make both Earth and Water tickled with joy.

The Minuses: The flip side of compatibility and togetherness is too much dependence on one another. An Earth/Water couple can fuse in an unhealthy way so that you no longer function well on your own. Mutual support is fine, but overdependence is counterproductive. When you rely on your partner to feel whole, you've bonded in a way that makes you weaker rather than stronger.

Earth is a natural caregiver and tends to worry a lot. Water is highly imaginative and can picture the bad along with the good. It's easy to see how they might sometimes envision worst-case scenarios. Earth and Water can become fearful about losing each other or something happening to one another. Again, this kind of anxiety can lead the Earth/Water couple to cling to each other in an unhealthy way.

Arguments usually surround Water's emotionalism or Earth's bullheadedness. If Earth won't budge on some practical matter, like paying the bills, but Water really wants to go out for dinner on a special day, then there's trouble in store. Water may need to realize that their happiness is not found in Earth's wallet, and Earth may need to give a little more.

The Challenge: While Earth admires Water's ability to feel deeply, sometimes Earth gets too much of a good thing. Earth reaches a saturation point and can't absorb any more of Water's emotionalism. At this point, Earth tunes out, and that's when Water's emotions kick into overdrive. Water hates to be avoided and will become even more emotional to get a response from Earth. How can you communicate to your partner that you need a break without hurting his or her feelings?

Suggestion: Give each other a massage. It doesn't have to be long, but you must have the best intentions. So grab some oil or body lotion and work on each other's shoulders, feet, or lower back. Go easy! This is not a contest. The idea is to find a spot that feels tense, and by keeping your hand there, it will relax. Ahhh!

In Private: Earth and Water are the most sensual pair, so expect a great bedroom experience! Water instinctively knows what feels good for Earth and is happy to oblige. Earth comes alive under Water's feel-good spell and follows Water's lead step by step. Earth is eager for a physical connection, and Water never disappoints. Even a sexual connection leaves the Earth/Water pair in a place of safety and satisfaction.

In Public: Earth and Water can express feelings for one another and bring these feelings to life in a tangible form. Other people consider you creative and expressive in everything, from the way you dress to how your home is decorated. It's your love of art that they see. Together, you are innovative and are willing to experiment with art and see how it moves you. You're the perfect pair to help with community theater, a school bake sale, or the children's reading period at the local library.

Some Earth/Water Advice

Dear Dr. Craig,

I am a stay-at-home housewife and mother, and a good one, if I do say so myself. My husband is a fine man. He's protective, sensitive, and great with the kids. When he tells a story, my jaw drops and my eyes pop. What an imagination! But his active imagination has been causing some trouble lately. I like to go out with my girlfriends once a month or so and unwind. When I get home, my husband probes me for every detail about where I went, whom I talked to, and what I did. Sometimes when we go out together, he imagines that another man is flirting with me and gets jealous. I don't notice a thing, but he thinks every guy in the place has eyes for me. I'm flattered that my husband still seems crazy about me, but sometimes he just drives me crazy. He can be so moody. He's happy one minute and feeling down the next. I've never given my husband a reason to doubt my loyalty. I'm getting tired of his jealousy. I hope you have some helpful advice.

—TRUSTY

Dear Trusty,

Of course you're busy at home; you're an Earth type. Keeping order is one of your special talents. And you deserve some time out. Staying in the house all the time can make anyone stir-crazy. Your husband is a classic Water type. He's protective and then takes it to the extreme. He's at the mercy of his emotions. Yes, he's temperamental. So you need to reassure him and keep him reassured. Tell him that it hurts when he doesn't trust you and that he should have no fear of losing you. I'll bet that's the problem. Also, tell him he can save that active imagination for better things, like remodeling the kitchen.

—DR. CRAIG

The Garden

Different couples respond to the same experience in different ways. Earth loves to build things and make things grow. What happens when Earth pairs up with other elements to create a backyard garden? Let's take a look.

Earth/Earth Couple: This garden is all about structure, organization, and order. The Earth/Earth couple loves to plan, and it shows. You're experts at making a list and creating a budget. You've compared prices and know which retailer has the best deal on sod, seed, fencing, and everything else you need. You really get into the details and understand soil mixtures, pH levels, fertilizer, mulch, and composting. For you, it's important to have the proper gardening tools so that you're sure to get things right. When you finish planting, you install stepping-stones that lead from your home to the garden. You may even put in a garden gnome to watch over it all.

Earth/Fire Couple: This garden reflects the Earth/Fire couple's vision and creativity. You want to create a one-of-a-kind backyard space that expresses your bold ideas. Fire envisions a spectacular garden, and Earth has the planning skills and follow-through to make it happen. Of course, when you're working in the garden, you need the right accessories: boots, clogs, gloves, and jackets in bright colors. After everything is in the ground, you string up Italian lights and install a sundial, and then crack open a bottle of cabernet and toast your handiwork.

Earth/Air Couple: This garden is eclectic and elegant. Earth and Air work well together to create something unusual and unexpected. Air loves variety and chooses out-of-the-ordinary plants that range from arugula to gazania. Air selects accessories like wind spinners, wind chimes, and bird feeders, while Earth takes time to make sure everything is in its place, all the plants have just the right solar exposure, and the chaise lounges are plush and ready to go. When it's all in full bloom, you love to sit back, have friends over, and talk about how gardening has enhanced your love life.

Earth/Water Couple: This garden is all about artistic expression and sensory stimulation. The Earth/Water couple creates a garden that's beautiful to the eye, delightful to the nose, sensual to the touch, and a pleasure for the taste buds. Birds sing while splashing in the birdbath you've installed, so your ears get enjoyment as well. When the garden blooms with life, it makes you feel peaceful, happy, and safe. Together, you've created a lovely spot where you can commune with nature and each other.

Part IV

Elemental Potential

18
Intimacy and Potential

Doing the honest, intimate work of a healthy relationship has an amazing effect on both you and your partner—individually and as a couple. Not only does it help your relationship work out and last, but it also brings with it the opportunity to achieve your potential, an admirable result for all your efforts.

Your potential is the possibility that you could act from your best self. Why would you want to do that? Because giving, caring, and acting from your best self makes you happy. And ignoring your potential only leads to misery.

Potential is a goal, not a state of being. It is something you work toward. It can't be expected that you will act from your potential all the time. Yet potential is something you strive for. You do this by making good choices. The good choices I'm referring to are the ones you make regarding your character. They are made through intimacy—love, honesty, and dynamic inner growth (DIG).

Your relationship is the best place for you to become more aware of yourself, the choices you make, and the effect those choices have on your partner. If you act badly, your partner will let you know. His or her reaction is a quick and direct way of seeing your choice. Hopefully, you care about their reaction and feelings, at least enough to look at what you've done. Without caring, you can't reach your potential.

Your potential is the possibility that
you could act from your best self.

Compassion

Compassion is the love and caring you have for your partner's well-being. It motivates you to make better choices in your relationship. Without compassion, you would be completely focused on yourself. In a relationship, you have to think about yourself, but you also have to focus on your partner and his or her needs too.

Compassion is more than just a passive feeling; it's a feeling that leads to action. You act from your potential because you care. Your best self comes forward and attempts to make things better.

Just like a hero, you can be inspired to act from your best self
because your partner needs you.

Caring in Action

A hero is an individual who lives up to his or her potential. When a hero sees someone in need, compassion compels them to act. This applies not only to superheroes and the heroes of Greek mythology; it applies to you too.

Just like a hero, you can be inspired to act from your best self because your partner needs you. You rise to the occasion with your potential and make difficult and selfless choices because you see his or her need and you care.

Caring as Example

You can also offer your potential as an example. You don't always have to rescue the baby from the burning building. Just by being yourself and acting from your potential, others can see, learn, and act from their potential too.

Setting an example offers only a possibility for someone else's growth. You can't force anyone to grow and meet their potential. But one thing's for sure: acting from your negative self does not help others grow.

Virtue and Potential

Many heroes can be found in Greek mythology. In fact, ancient Greek thought dealt extensively with human potential. In ancient thought, and even in modern psychology, there is the concept of human virtue. Loosely, you could think of that as "the best in yourself," or your individual potential.

Each elemental style has a particular potential of its own, with compassion at its heart. Those potentials are described in ancient Greek philosophy as the virtues. There are four of them. I think it's worth taking a look at the ancient virtues because even though we rarely refer to them by their old names, they are still the highest points of human potential even today.

Ancient Greek philosophy defined the four virtues of mankind as fortitude, justice, temperance, and prudence. For the purposes of making them more modern, I am going to call them strength, truth, moderation, and wisdom. The meanings remain the same, but the modern language may make them more understandable and easier to apply to yourself. Each virtue corresponds to one of the four elements in elemental psychology.

THE FOUR HUMAN VIRTUES

GREEK VIRTUE	MODERN POTENTIAL	ELEMENT	WHAT IS IT?
Fortitude	Strength	Fire	Inner conviction—the ability to stand in the face of adversity
Justice	Truth	Air	Fairness—the ability to know the difference between right and wrong
Temperance	Moderation	Water	Balance—the ability to remain centered
Prudence	Wisdom	Earth	Understanding—the ability to apply knowledge from experience

As your deeper needs are met, you will discover that they are linked with your potential.

Your Elemental Potential

In the chapter that follows, we will look at how your elemental style connects you with the four virtues. This is the path to your own "best self." Discovering your potential through the positive effect you can have on your partner and the people around you is awesome. It is not something that you find easily, but most things that have lasting value aren't easy.

As your deeper needs are met, you will discover that they are linked with your potential. You become aware that intimacy and dynamic inner growth (DIG) make good choices possible. So being in a great relationship that meets those needs brings you a giant step closer to attaining your highest good.

19
Your Elemental Potential

Each elemental style has a unique potential. Knowing your style helps you express that potential in your relationship and the world around you. As a loving person, you want to see your behavior have a positive effect on the people in your life. It feels good to see yourself acting as your best self. When you choose to act with compassion, you approach your potential. To care or not to care, that is the question.

So, let's look at your elemental potential. In the pages that follow, I've shown each element as divided into three different aspects. These three facets are a beginning. There are no limits and there is always room to grow. Potential is a target that we aim for, a score we seek to best. Through your relationship, love, and a desire to grow, you can glimpse and achieve your potential and more.

When you choose to act with compassion,
you approach your potential.

— ◊ ☁ ☼ ⚘ —

Fire

Fire's potential is strength, or fortitude. This doesn't mean physical strength. Strength of character is Fire's virtue. Strength of character has many aspects. Let's look at leadership, sharing, and positivity as three forms of strength that Fire style can exemplify.

Leadership

When you have the strength to lead, you stand up for your beliefs and show others the way. You lead by being a role model, listening, and inspiring action in others. Leadership is the choice to inspire or encourage rather than dominate. In a relationship where your partner wants to lose a few pounds, your encouragement gives your partner the opportunity to do it for him- or herself, rather than demands, which only serves your need to control.

Sharing

The strength of sharing is the ability to give something of meaning to others. Usually for Fire, what gets shared is some part of you and your energy. Sharing is the choice to be generous and supportive rather than selfish or hogging. When you've thrown a dinner party as a couple and a guest compliments just you, instead of taking all the glory and basking in it, you say, "We both put it together. I couldn't have done it alone."

Positivity

Being positive is the strength of hope and faith. It is the ability to bring optimism out of dark places. Positivity is the choice to be positive and confident in others rather than negative or belittling. In your relationship, let's assume you're the fantastic cook and your partner's not, but your partner wants to try his or her hand at a new recipe. It's better to be positive that your partner can do it rather than belittle them for fear that you'll get shown up.

Fire's Strength

By acting from a place of leadership, sharing, and positivity, Fire shows his or her potential. When you connect with compassion and care for your partner, it's easy to find Fire's strength.

Air

Air's potential is truth, or justice. This doesn't mean courts or cops. Truth of personal integrity is Air's virtue. Truth of personal integrity has many aspects. Let's look at simplicity, diplomacy, and impartiality as three forms of truth that the Air style can exemplify.

Simplicity

The simple truth is all it takes. But it seems so hard to find. Simplicity is the choice to communicate directly and simply rather than use complex language to hide the truth. In your relationship, making excuses for bad behavior is the most common way that the truth gets hidden in complicated language. Rather than just saying, "Yes, I was smoking," and accepting the consequences, you might think it's easier to tell a whole story about how a cigarette mysteriously landed in your mouth. Well, it's not easier.

Diplomacy

Diplomacy is truth because it honors both sides of a situation. It is the truth of deal making and having everyone feel good about an outcome. Diplomacy is the choice to compromise rather than remain steadfast in your opinion. You and your partner could be painting the bedroom and voicing ideas of what colors look best. Perhaps you want to paint it yellow, but your partner wants to paint it blue; the truth of what looks best for you both might look closer to green.

Impartiality

The truth of impartiality happens when we review all the information at hand before making a decision. It is the ability to stand apart from a situation and observe. Impartiality is the choice to remain objective rather than take sides and align with an idea for selfish purposes. When you're looking to buy a car with your partner and you've agreed that good gas mileage is your top priority, then perhaps that sports car you've had your eye on won't meet up to the standards of truth.

Air's Truth

By acting from a place of simplicity, diplomacy, and impartiality, Air shows its potential. When you connect with compassion and care for your partner, it's easy to find Air's truth.

Water

Water's potential is moderation, or temperance. This doesn't mean rehab. Emotional self-control is Water's virtue. Emotional self-

control has many aspects. Let's look at nurturing, transformation, and composure as three forms of moderation that Water style can exemplify.

Nurturing

Moderation is found in nurturing because you act from the midpoint between push and pull. Nurturing is the choice to simultaneously encourage and protect rather than stifle, suffocate, or exploit. In your relationship, let's assume that your partner wants to go back to school. When you nurture his or her desire to grow, you reinforce your partner's decision for more education as a good choice. You honor their desire for achievement, and you look out for them rather than suppress him or her with your own fears.

Transformation

Transformation is a slow and delicate process. It requires moderation to allow change to happen in its own way and time. Transformation is a choice to catalyze change rather than force change before its ready. When you have an argument with your partner, time is needed before you can come back together and work it out. The time that is necessary for change to occur is different for everyone. In order to transform the situation back to a loving, happy union, you need to know when someone is ready to talk. Forcing your relationship to work out is not going to work out.

Composure

When you think before you speak, it takes moderation. By collecting yourself and being composed, you can respond rather than react. Composure is the choice to express your feelings while considering what effect they have on your partner rather than expressing yourself immediately without any thoughts of the impact of your actions. Perhaps in your relationship, your feelings get hurt and you'd like to resort to name-calling. By collecting your feelings first and stopping yourself from hurting your partner in return, you prevent the escalation of more emotional drama.

Water's Moderation

By acting from a place of nurturing, transformation, and composure, Water shows its potential. When you connect with compassion and care for your partner, it's easy to find Water's potential.

Earth

Earth's potential is wisdom—not the wisdom of lost scrolls but the wisdom of experience is Earth's virtue. Wisdom of experience has many aspects. Let's look at value, determination, and planning as three forms of wisdom that Earth style can exemplify.

Value

Knowing the value of something or someone is wise. It takes wisdom to see beyond the face value of something and truly see its inner worth. Value is a choice to find importance in all things rather than discarding something as worthless. It is looking beyond the surface and seeing the merit in something. In your relationship, a partner who is kind might be of more value than a partner with lots of money. Likewise, an honest partner might be of more value than one with great looks. Let the wisdom of value decide!

Determination

When we stick with something, we push through resistance and find something of worth. Being determined is having the wisdom to not give up. Determination is the choice to apply your energy for tangible and positive results rather than being lazy and running at the least bit of trouble. In the relationship, when you've committed to helping repair the bathroom floor, your determination to complete the job, even when it's tougher than expected, and will earn you all the gratitude you deserve.

Planning

When you want something to last, you plan. You plan even when you just want something to go more smoothly. Planning is wise because it gives you life goals and markers to achieve. Planning is the choice to think things out and be meticulous rather than sloppy or slipshod. Going on a special holiday weekend away with your partner and not planning motel reservations will probably not turn out to be the wisest thing you've ever done.

Earth's Wisdom

By acting from a place of value, determination, and planning, Earth shows its potential. When you connect with compassion and care for your partner, it's easy to find Earth's wisdom.

No matter what your elemental style,
your potential is beautiful.

A Small Step

Making choices from your potential is possible. They are not easy choices to make. Being domineering, insensitive, moody, or rigid is behavior that protects you from feeling hurt. The qualities on your laundry list don't just go away because you recognize them. By making small steps toward being your best self, your relationship can grow with intimacy, honesty, and love.

20
The Lover's Journey

The road trip of love goes on. There is no end point to what you can learn about yourself or your partner. All the things you've agreed upon, such as how fast to go and where you're headed, are in place. With love, honesty, and a desire to grow, you're all set for a long, long ride. And now that you understand your deeper needs for love, you increase the possibility of happiness in your relationship.

The lover's journey is about opening yourself up. It is about casting a wider net, not limiting yourself to superficial beliefs, and embracing the internal change that love inevitably brings to your life. It is an honest journey toward discovering your needs and attracting the person who meets those needs. And that's just the beginning.

By really taking a look at who someone is, you know if the person can meet your needs. You become more willing to share those needs because you have someone to trust, and it feels so good to get your needs met.

Your relationship is still going to require work, but it is fun too. In any good relationship, you'll have to do dynamic inner growth (DIG) work to make the partnership last. Beyond that is the happiness that all this work leads to.

When you are essentially happy in your relationship—that is, when your needs are met—doing the work won't be so hard. It's actually a joy to watch it work out. Everything you get from your special someone is what you've been looking for all along.

As your journey unfolds, you learn that love is not about relationship drama anymore. It's about happiness. You end up truly happy because you have someone who meets your needs, encourages you to feel good about yourself, and brings out the best in you.

You get there by working out your stuff together. Someone you can do your laundry with is a good someone to find. You make space for each other to experience personal challenges. Combined, you become a great team, and the love only grows.

When you are essentially happy in your relationship—that is, when your needs are met—doing the work won't be so hard.

As time goes on, the journey deepens because you keep doing the work. You keep growing, and your partner does too. Rather than ignore or dismiss difficulties, you address them and grow further. The love you share reinforces this process and, at the same time, increases that love. By finding someone who meets your deeper needs, you can be in a truly intimate relationship—one that encourages your personal inner growth and guides you toward your potential.

In the end, you watch yourself react with love. This brings with it all the patience, understanding, compassion, and dignity that love provides. The journey toward meeting your deeper needs together becomes your story of love. It's the story of a love that works and a relationship that works out.

Appendices

Appendix 1

THE DEEPER NEEDS

FIRE	AIR	WATER	EARTH
Control	Truth	Reassurances	Stability
Recognition	Freedom	Understanding	Reliability
Praise	Mental stimulation	Imagination	Security
Admiration from others	Feeling unrestricted	Being emotionally validated	Having hands-on experience
Being able to get their way	Valuing friendship	Feeling safe to express	Comfort of body and mind
Making decisions for themselves	Being lighthearted	Need for "alone time"	Being financially secure
Being the focal point	Having community and interaction	Connection to home	Reliability of others

Appendix 11

THE CHOICE

FIRE	AIR	WATER	EARTH
Having to be important	Having to be stimulated	Having to be cared for	Having to be secure
Kindness vs. intimidation	Focused vs. scattered	Affectionate vs. manipulative	Generous vs. greedy
The Wizard from *The Wizard of Oz*	The White Rabbit from *Alice in Wonderland*	Tinkerbell from *Peter Pan*	Scrooge from *A Christmas Carol*

VULNERABILITY

FIRE	AIR	WATER	EARTH
Not feeling admired	Feeling restricted	Feeling uncared for	Feeling ungrounded
Not getting their way	Being heavy	Feeling crazy	Feeling financial stress
Having others make decisions that affect them	Having to focus	Having a lack of safe space	Being physically uncomfortable
Not being the center of attention	Feeling without community	Feeling disconnected from "home"	Having people be unreliable

DEFENSIVENESS

FIRE	AIR	WATER	EARTH
Intimidating	Unavailable	Manipulative	Withdrawn
Accusatory	Evasive	Hysterical	Stubborn
Righteous	Spacey	Martyred	Petty
Combative	Scattered	Begrudging	Dogmatic

DYNAMIC INNER GROWTH (DIG) PATTERN

ELEMENT	CHALLENGED BY	PREOCCUPIED WITH	DIG OCCURS WITH
Fire	Arrogance Forcefulness Entitlement Superiority	Self-importance	Humility Gentleness
Air	Aloofness Distractibility Superficiality Being unfocused	Stimulation	Sensitivity Focus
Water	Casting blame Escapism Moodiness Clinging	Bonding	Trust Moderation
Earth	Rigidity Restriction Materialism Reserve	Stability	Flexibility Charity

SPACE FOR INTROSPECTION

FIRE	AIR	WATER	EARTH
Crafts	Journaling	Music	Exercise
Sports	Reading	Dance	Gardening
Personal challenges	Affirmation	Motion	Handiwork
Nature	Laughing	Visualization	Housework
			Creating order

NEEDS SOMEONE WHO CAN HANDLE

FIRE	AIR	WATER	EARTH
Their demanding and domineering attitude	Their talkativeness and scattered attitude	Their moodiness and unrealistic attitude	Their stubbornness and appearance orientation
Someone who will let them take charge	Someone who will let them be free and who likes their sense of humor	Someone who will let them express themselves and make space for their feelings and dreams	Someone who will let them be organized, regimented, habitual, and financially responsible

EXPRESSIONS OF INTIMACY—THE APOLOGY

FIRE	AIR	WATER	EARTH
Compliments	Emails	Poems	Gifts
Surprises	Letters	Music	Chores
Generosity	Phone calls	CDs and DVDs	Helpfulness
Supportiveness	Words	Cards with feeling	Back rubs

Appendix III

ELEMENTAL QUALITIES

FIRE	AIR	WATER	EARTH
Enthusiastic	Diplomatic	Imaginative	Responsible
Original	Eccentric	Nurturing	Prudent
Exciting	Keen	Sensitive	Productive
Generous	Quick-witted	Artistic	Patient
Outgoing	Stimulating	Meditative	Trustworthy
Competitive	Animated	Emotional	Industrious
Ambitious	Graceful	Sympathetic	Reliable
Impulsive	Wise	Intuitive	Dependable
Creative	Abounding with ideas	Emotive	Practical
Passionate		Compassionate	Realistic
Center of attention	Intelligent	Sensitive	Persistent
	Language skills	Caring	Respectful
Motivational	Communicative	Empathic	Hardworking
Charming	Intellectual	Romantic	Loyal
Warm	Alert	Supportive	Serious
Starring role	Adaptable	Penetrating	Secure
Assertive	Flexible	Protective	Stable
Leadership	Stimulating	Affectionate	Traditional
Bold	Curious	Introverted	Fastidious
Extroverted	Fair	Receptive	Self-reliant
Fun-loving	Persuasive	Contemplative	Organized
Confident	Independent	Poetic	Confident
Courageous	Freedom-loving		Scholarly

Continued on next page

Continued from previous page

FIRE	AIR	WATER	EARTH
Energetic	Astute	Dreamy	Upright
Kind	Versatile	Responsive	Generous
Giving	Sharp	Inspirational	Steady
Innovative	Funny	Charismatic	Slow to anger
Big impression	Humorous	Musical	Dutiful
Adventurous	Vivacious	Psychic	Perseverant
Positive	Talkative	Intense	Tenacious
Resourceful	Articulate	Perceptive	Ambitious
Frank	Popular	Domestic	Enduring
	Social	Nostalgic	Conforming
	Group-oriented	Sacrificing	Cautious
	Agile	Mystical	
	Clever	Tender	
	Inquisitive		

DIG WORK QUALITIES:
THE LAUNDRY LIST (CHALLENGES)

FIRE	AIR	WATER	EARTH
Demanding	Unreliable	Jealous	Meticulous
Impetuous	Narrow-minded	Smothering	Timid
Domineering	Distrustful	Lazy	Obstinate
Obstinate	Suspicious	Escapist	Petty
Intolerant	Fickle	Addicted	Greedy
Argumentative	Unpredictable	Unrealistic	Extravagant
Bossy	Discouraging	Immature	Rigid
Righteous	Bitter	Hysterical	Inflexible
Egotistical	Devious	Moody	Materialistic
Exaggerating	Unfair	Martyred	Stubborn
Quarrelsome	Cold	Grudge-holding	Reserved
Combative	Aloof	Impenetrable	Limited
Audacious	Inconstant	Self-destructive	Limiting
Haughty	Superficial	Wastes time	Unyielding
Arrogant	High-strung	Spoiled	Fears change
Boastful	Vain	Deceptive	Fussy
Temperamental	Meddlesome	Sullen	Spend and hoard
Accusatory	Distracted	Resentful	Wasteful
Pushy	Insensitive	Sarcastic	Dogmatic
Aggressive	Dismissive	Depressed	Stagnant
Pompous	Nervous		

Appendix IV

ELEMENTAL POTENTIALS

FIRE	AIR	WATER	EARTH
Strength:	**Truth:**	**Moderation:**	**Wisdom:**
Leadership	Simplicity	Nurturing	Value
Sharing	Diplomacy	Transformation	Determination
Positivity	Impartiality	Composure	Planning